Doing Good with Money

MICHAEL GORDON

DOING GOOD with MONEY

How We Can All Make a Difference

Restoring Communities and Building Relationships

© 2023 Michael Gordon

Published by Michael Gordon
https://profmichaelgordon.com

Cover, layout, and editioral by Dean Bargh, Witchwood Production House
http://www.witchwoodhouse.com

ISBN-13: 978-0-9882114-3-8 [paperback]
ISBN-13: 978-0-9882114-4-5 [PDF ebook]
ISBN-13: 978-0-9882114-5-2 [ePub ebook]

Contents

Acknowledgments

Thanks to everyone who's helped me with this book.

I've had a lot of help, starting with students. They were the first to hear some of the ideas in this book, which they debated with me, and always provided me a sense of hope that we *can* "do good" in the world, with money and otherwise. Thanks to you all.

I want to give a few students my special thanks: Charlene Franke spoke with me over and over again about low-income financial institutions (CDFIs); Harika Kolluri did a lot of legwork digging into carbon credits; Vedika Aigalikar and Sanghamithra Kalima offered important observations about "emergence"; Taylor Hurley was an amazing source of support and insight when I taught my course "Finance for Societal Good"; Avery Conybeare, Ashley Gorman, Annie Ryan, and I formed a book group that read about serious social issues, and they also helped me see the world as my readers might; Britta Holum and I had many conversations about climate finance and other things; and, finally, India Solomon and I had many conversations related to making the world better and helping me clarify my thinking.

Thank you all.

(And then there are more . . . I'm so sorry I forgot to mention you. But *please* know I valued your contribution and support.)

Two students deserve extra special attention and thanks: I had the pleasure of spending more than a year talking with Pooja Subramaniam, who linked what I was writing with moral philosophy and helped me flesh out almost every idea I was thinking. Lindsey Masterman assisted me for more than six months when this book was "almost done"; her careful (re-)reading and commentary helped me actually get "done." Thank you both.

I've been blessed by many practitioners in the money-meets-impact world who graciously joined my class for a few hours as guest speakers. There are so many of you, and I've never kept a list. Let me thank some of you: Steve Hollingworth, Karen Biddle Andres, Marc Gunther, Katherine Lynch, Michael Shuman, Mark Newberg, Oran Hesterman, Jean Chorazyczewski, Jim Davidson, Tiffany Talsma, Jonathan Lewis, Kristin Hull, Matthew Patsky, Angela Barbash, Andy Lower, Evelina Fredriksson, Keith McCandless, Fisher Qua, Moira Birss, Babita Patel, Steven Atamian, Rahul Brown, Corrina Grace, Bela Shah, and Ruchi Varma.

Other friends with whom I've shared and explored some of these ideas are: Linda Barterian, Perry Samson, Julie Woodward, George Abrahams, Kerri Lake, Sheryn Brown, Ruth Pittard, Cynthia Koenig, John Kinyon, Simon Wiskowski, Lora Vatalaro, and Ruth Lopez. Thank you for your friendship.

When I was actively writing my newsletter, a number of readers commented in ways that were helpful (asking a question, providing clarification) and fun (letting me know how they were applying ideas I was talking about). My most avid reader and commenter is my friend Dave Law.

The person with whom I've gone deepest with most of my thoughts about values, money, and community is Paul Karsten, who shows me a different world on a weekly basis.

Thanks to Dean Bargh of Witchwood Production House, for helping me clarify my thoughts and providing, with great care and friendship, all the tech skills from editing through production which went into this book.

A group that has influenced much of my thinking in latter drafts of this book is ServiceSpace.org, which embraces life's interconnectedness, acting with generosity, and each of us doing our part. It's been an honor and a pleasure getting to know so many of you.

Thank you to Candace for all the love, fun, and companionship we share. To Hannah and Molly, I love you too.

Introduction

DOING GOOD WITH MONEY

Money is nowadays understood as the engine of human civilization. The "economy" — an all-compassing word that defies a definition we can all agree on — seems the god of the modern age that demands sacrifices to sustain it. Money is a barometer of success, the metric by which all things are valued; it is our daily math woven into our lives. And we can all see its destructive power when humans pursue it ruthlessly for its own sake. We can choose to disdain it, to see it as nothing more than a metaphor for exchange — but we can't avoid it. But if it's so pervasive and so powerful, what can we achieve when we harness it for good? Maybe we have all been turned into "consumers" these days; well, if that's the case, then it's in our pocketbooks where our power lies. And you, individual reader, have more power than you think.

This is a book about how you — we, all of us, not just the super-wealthy — can use our money as a tool for good.

Lots of books will tell you how to make money, how to save money, how to stretch a dollar, how to invest, or how to grow your money in a myriad other ways, from the mundane to the bordering on crazy. But, when so much is a stake in the world, what about *doing good with money*? Including the money you have right now. The money you will be spending next month on all the regular stuff.

Do you need to be a professional "do-gooder" to do good with money? Do you have to be retired? Or old? Do you need to have a lot of money? Does doing good with money have to be your main concern? The answer to all these questions is no. I say this as a former professor whose focus in working with students, colleagues, and practitioners the last two decades has been on just that: *doing good with money*.

The hardest move for any of us is to turn intention into action. This is therefore a *practical* book that will guide you into putting your toe in the water — to start doing some good with the money that you have. I hope it makes you think about using money with greater intention. To see money as a tool for inclusion, generosity, and fairness. And to see ourselves moving toward a system aligned with societal good.

I don't think anyone has a corner on precisely how to do good with money (including me). But please bear with me. I offer a perspective, developed over quite some time as I've thought about the relationship between money and society. My perspective may be different from yours, but my main goal is to provide a useful starting point for anyone hoping the find their way through this range of issues.

Money has come to mean power — certainly power *over* — but it was not always thought of in this way, and maybe we can refashion our thinking to make it serve our needs — *the whole planet's true needs* — more faithfully. *Doing good with money* quite simply expresses the possibility that we can pursue societal good by the ways in which we use our money. This book discusses what those ways are: the various areas of your financial life in which a behavior change can benefit wider society — your spending, your savings, your investing, and your charitable giving. (Notwithstanding the book's title, sometimes the best way to do good with money might be to dispense with it — if a money-less way of engaging can bring us closer together than an economic transaction would. That idea, too, will be explored in these pages.)

But *doing good with money* immediately raises a question: What is "good?" To answer that question means invoking values. Values, of course, are personal, yet some are widely shared and seem more or less fundamental to pro-social behavior: kindness, compassion, generosity, consideration of other people's needs, looking for what we have in common rather than how we differ, being there for each other, being humble in the face of all we don't understand. At least, that makes for a pretty neat summary of the values that underlie this book's approach to doing good with money.

Different value systems can employ different logics. For instance, we can examine charitable giving via an economic/mathematical lens, or we may embrace the internal logic of "following our hearts." I treat both perspectives as valid and possible. For other topics that also attract differing and yet useful perspectives, I will not exclude one in favor of another. There are many different ways of seeing the world.

This book is being published at an unusual moment in time. When I began writing it pre-Covid, I couldn't have imagined the world as it is today, as I add these final lines in mid-2022: a world struggling to emerge from a pandemic, with millions of lives lost; a world horrified to witness a police officer kneeling on a man's neck, snuffing out his life.

But, in fact, it is hard to see it as a single world — one in which clashing ideas are respectfully debated — but rather plural worlds with vastly different realities based on different "truths." And always the ominous drumbeat in the background: rising temperatures, ferocious storms, uncontrollable fires, and all the tragedies we have come to know too well, hurtling us toward a climate cliff of our own making.

It is against such a background that this book, I hope, brings an important message, both practical and hopeful. It is *our* decisions, *our* actions, what *we* believe and value — these underlie change. Our behavior plants seeds of change and inspires others to join us. Beyond today's chaos is the world that is emerging. This may be the moment, much more than ever before, to take action — for the planet and for each other.

And there follows now a crucial point, which many of us need to hear. Faced with what seem like insurmountable problems and forces (corporate and natural) beyond our control, many of us are deterred from action by a sense of helplessness. We feel that the challenges are so huge that our actions as individuals are insignificant — "what's the point?" Please read on, and be inspired by the myriad initiatives underway which are doing significant good *now* and which we can be a part of. Read Chapter 1, which provides a strategy for making the first steps. And, particularly, read Chapter 11 and learn about the power of *emergence* and see how system change may arise, where each one of us has a role to play.

We choose the future we focus on. When we're at our best, we're already living it.

Note

I began writing this book pre-Covid and finished rewriting it (for the last time) post-Covid (if indeed that's a valid description of the moment we are in now). You may notice passages that reflect this (things like: talking about flying as if there were no public health danger, and also talking about how Covid reduced the number of air passengers by 95% early in the pandemic,[1] resulting in less CO_2 pouring into the skies). I've retained both perspectives because, to me, we're in a state of flux — the "new normal" won't be the "old normal." If you notice these shifts, now you'll understand how they arose.

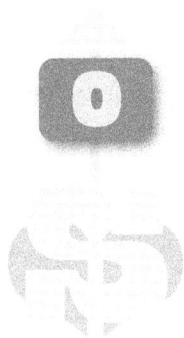

YOU ARE HERE

Now that you have this book (or device) in your hands, you might ask yourself, should I read it straight through from beginning to end? That's how I wrote it, so please go ahead.

But that's not the only way to read — or use — this book. You see, first of all I want to give you practical advice about "how to do good with money." But a lot of the ideas might seem initially familiar, so I also want to give you some deeper context. For instance, you have probably heard about fair trade or "local" purchasing movements. But there is a lot to find out about — more than slogans or simple answers. So my goal is to provide enough detail so that you have a clearer picture of the issues when you're wondering about how exactly to "do good with money."

That's not the fastest way of getting to the heart of my advice, of course. So, if you want to go straight to specific recommendations, look for the takeaways at the end of each chapter. And there are some useful appendices listing tools and information you can apply directly. (But please remember: like I just said, there's more to this than meets the eye. That's why this book exists.)

Please continue to explore some enlightening and surprising perspectives on something that is at once familiar and yet broadly misunderstood, and to find different ways of *doing good with money*.

1 GIVE IT YOUR 15%

Now, in 2022, we can at least agree what are the major problems facing the world right now.

Covid struck when this book was well underway. I began recording statistics from the Johns Hopkins Coronavirus Resource Center. In April 2020: 4¾ million confirmed cases worldwide; in July 2020: 17 million cases; by early September: nearly 27 million cases . . . And now, the figure stands at over 600 million confirmed cases, including more than 1 million reported deaths in the U.S. alone, and estimates of at least 10 times that number worldwide. This once-in-a-century pandemic, which has wreaked havoc on all parts of our lives, may be the beginning of a new normal, according to many experts.

NASA lists the consequences of what we're doing to the Earth: oceans are warming (absorbing 90% of the additional heat unleashed by the climate crisis), ice sheets are melting (three times faster than before in the Antarctic), glaciers are in retreat (in the Himalayas 40% of the ice will be gone by the end of the century), sea levels are rising (4–8 feet within 80 years, flooding up to 5% of the planet every year), the ocean is becoming more acidic (threatening up to 90% of coral reefs, which supply food for half a billion people), and extreme weather events are becoming almost common-place. Floods, droughts, food shortages, and refugees escaping temperatures too intense for life will follow.[2] In the most recent climate report by the Intergovernmental Panel on Climate Change, the leading authority on climate change, we learn (italics mine):

> Human-induced climate change, including more frequent and intense extreme events, has caused widespread adverse impacts and related losses and *damages to nature* and people ... [T]he most vulnerable people and systems are observed to be disproportionately affected. The rise in weather and climate extremes has led to some *irreversible impacts as natural and human systems are pushed beyond their ability to adapt.* (high confidence).[3]

As we know all too well, we can add any number of other problems to this list, including: poverty, discrimination, polarization, misinformation, attacks on democracy, war, plague, gun violence, ... the list goes on. Each of these deserves our attention. How can we respond, and how can we choose which issues to respond to, when the problems are both enormous and so plentiful? One way is *not* to give it our all. Follow another approach: 15% solutions. Let me explain.

There are many things we might do, but the enormity of it all can paralyze us into inaction. A 15%-solutions approach acknowledges this and reassures us that we **don't have to do it all**. "I'll focus on the environment, not healthcare."

"I'll protect giant pandas before Galapagos penguins." A 15% approach puts us in motion. We can act now, and then continue as new opportunities arise.

Even though problems are huge, we can start small, in our own lives. We don't need to aim at a too-distant target. Our own, small universe can provide opportunities to offer our support. Those acts can help bring out the best in ourselves. Although 15% may only be part of the way there, that part takes us a long way. Start small; see what happens.

A 15% solution does not demand a total reconfiguration of your life. You don't need to stop driving and flying, become a vegan, or join the Peace Corps. You don't need to renounce having fun, or move to a cave. We can use a 15%-solutions approach to set limits to our endeavors: make 15% of our investments impact investments, for example; or devote 15% of our free time to volunteering. We *can* do something. We don't need to do *every*thing.

- 15% is kind of a nice number.
- 15% of a marathon is almost 4 miles.
- 15% of a pint is still a few gulps of beer.
- 15% of a week is one day.
- 15% of a work day is more than an hour.

What might happen when we take a 15% approach to addressing societal problems?

It may lead to significant change. Google, in its early days, allowed its workers to dedicate 20% of their time to personal projects. That's how the enormously popular Gmail and Google Maps were born. If we all dedicate 15% of our time, attention, or resources to societal good, there is an enormous amount of good we might do. Especially when we are joined by like-minded others.

Fifteen per cent might seem tentative, small. But first steps can be hard to take. We can take them, learn; let them become our path. Look deeper, and we may find connections we didn't know were there: public health is economic health; business can be generous; you can act local and think global.

Maybe 15% is as far as you ever go. That's OK: don't let the perfect be the enemy of the good. Small efforts aggregate into something truly significant (see Chapter 11).

As you read these pages, some suggestions might inspire you while others might leave you indifferent or even questioning my advice. What inspires you can become *your* 15% solution. There are small things right in front of each one of us that we can do now — to "do real good" with money. And, in the process, change ourselves as well.

Takeaways from this chapter

Life is complex; you're busy; no one can do it all. So pick something — some problem you're interested in or place you care about — and allocate a portion of your time, effort, or money to make it better. Say 15%, for a start.

BE
RECIPROCAL

Each summer, 70,000 people descend upon Black Rock City, Nevada, to attend the Burning Man festival. Each year, a miniature city is built to serve festival-goers' needs and desires — and just as quickly disassembled at the festival's end. During a recent summer, one of those festival-goers was Paul Romer, an economist who had won the Nobel Prize the year before. His interest lay in the makeshift city itself. Its layout, he believed, held clues for creating inclusive, economically and environmentally sustainable growth in Africa and Asia, and for instructing countries in the Global North on how to absorb massive migrations of people fleeing the climate crisis.

Burning Man's economy is based on reciprocity — where the "currency" of exchange can be a hug, singing a song, or a Beyond Burger; no money changes hands. A "reciprocal economy" is gentler than one based on barter.

Reciprocity doesn't require you to keep strict track of who owes whom what or how much. It's not even tit-for-tat, where I give something to you so you must return the favor. Rather, reciprocity is based on an expectation that, in my time of need, someone will step up, just as I will when I am able to provide for someone else. It's a notion that has served various societies well, including Native American Iroquois tribes, not just festival-goers. Under this philosophy, sharing is a form of communal activity that lifts everyone up.

Reciprocal exchange stands in stark contrast to the kind of economics we've been conditioned to since at least the eighteenth century, when Adam Smith argued that sellers should unsentimentally try to sell their goods for as much as possible while buyers aim for the opposite. (What's more, Smith argued, these *self*-interested actions are the best way to create a world serving *every*one. While merely *wishful*, this logic remains prevalent; and it motivates and is used to justify all sorts of selfish economic behavior.)

No economist would suggest that we create an economy based on hugs, music, or food. But reciprocity, as an ideal, attempts to repair some of the flaws in the "real" economy where companies (and people) operate in win–lose, isolating, self-protective ways. Reciprocity — in *practice* — takes many forms, each an example of what people- and nature-centered economics look like.

Reciprocity tilts the scales to help meet people's needs. We can see this in small actions. Karma Kitchen is a string of volunteer-run international restaurants. Each serves you a meal for free, while you "pay it forward" — however much you like — for future diners you will never meet. Karma Kitchen has restaurants in Detroit, Bangalore, Tokyo, and Jakarta, to name a few cities. Despite surface differences, each is an experiment in generosity. Karma Kitchen embraces reciprocity's economic logic: if everyone offers from their heart, everyone can live well. (In Chapter 12, "Meditation on My Own Book," we'll touch on what this might look like as an organizing principle.)

Even as a nation, our impulse is toward fairness and economic inclusion: we'd prefer wealth to be spread around much more evenly than it is now. Americans vastly underestimate how badly wealth is concentrated in this country. But, in experiments in which countries' names are masked, we overwhelmingly prefer how wealth is divided in Sweden (where it is much more equal) than in the United States. In fact, we'd like wealth to be divided in more evenly than that. This is true for about 90% of Americans, regardless of political party, gender, or level of income.[4]

Burning Man, Karma Kitchen, and national wealth operate on different scales, but their stories harmonize: people sharing, doing for others, and considering others' wellbeing alongside their own. Each example suggests that we can interact and share in ways so that everyone can enjoy a good life. Each places a higher priority on a group — even society — than on individuals, especially those who already have great advantages. Each recognizes the kind of wellbeing you get when those in a community take care of one another.

In principle, when I give you something and you give something back to me, that's reciprocity. Buying something at a hardware store fits that definition of reciprocity, but not necessarily its spirit. Buying things is ordinarily less about supporting each other and more about looking out for our own best interests. So is there a better definition of reciprocity?

The definition remains blurry. Say you do something nice for me and then later "call in" the favor. You began by acting with generosity (or kindness), and now you trust I'll be there for you. The idea that we'll be there for each other is a key component of the true idea of reciprocity, even though the back-and-forth nature of the exchange might superficially seem like a store transaction. Let's briefly look at a few other examples of reciprocity.

It doesn't have to involve just two parties — "you" and "me." We can visualize reciprocity as a circle: one member gives to another, who gives to another, who gives to another, . . . , who gives to the first. What you get in return for what you give is indirect. That is the idea behind "pay it forward" at Karma Kitchen: you do well by someone, who does well by someone, and so on, in ways you'll never see. But, as the effects of these acts ripple outward, the world may become a bit more generous and caring, and that does benefit you.

There are other ways in which we act with reciprocity without realizing it. For example: choosing to buy locally can help a school system (as we will see later). Choosing the right bank can help people buy homes in their communities. And choosing the right credit card might help stave off the worst effects of the climate crisis. In each of these examples (and others which we will see), taking a step to help someone else can produce ripples that return to support you. Even when you don't see them directly.

Much of the rest of this book is about choices. Doing good with money often means choosing to act with reciprocity, because forging a better world requires acting beyond ourselves.

Before I end this chapter, let's take a look at an example: a business that embraces the idea of reciprocity with the full intention of being the best neighbor it can possibly be.

Judy Wicks founded the White Dog Café in 1983, which she still runs and which has become one of the most complete examples anywhere of a local, "living" business (local business is the topic of Chapter 4). The establishment now takes in more than $5 million a year, but revenue or profit have never been her primary motivation. She attributes her success "to making decisions not for the sake of maximizing profits but instead maximizing relationships with our customers and staff, with our community, with our suppliers, and our natural environment".[5] Making decisions in the common interest is easy, she notes, "because I see the people [and environment] affected by my decisions."

Her life's experience has fed her imagination about what a local business might become: she has deep roots to place, which extend back 300 years to her ancestors arriving in Pennsylvania from Europe. As a young woman, she witnessed unlimited community generosity first hand at a "seal party" in Alaska, where a successful hunter's family divides up seal meat evenly among the community's members, and then also gives away any possessions the family doesn't absolutely need. She became aware of the horrendous living conditions of the pigs that would become White Dog Café bacon — and then stopped serving pork entirely until she could find a (more) humane source. When she saw the land she loved becoming parched due to climate change, White Dog Café's response was to become the first business in Pennsylvania to get all its electricity from windmills.

The White Dog Café, she explains, is "one small, very special restaurant" — built to be inextricably part of the area's local food system. Its menu boasts items that are trucked in from short distances away: produce, meats, even cheese, yogurt, and wine. Its suppliers check the right boxes for anyone concerned about sustainable food production: organic, free range, and the like. (If she can't purchase something like coffee locally, she buys fair trade — the topic of Chapter 4, "Stay Home.") The White Dog Café brings citizens together through dialogue on topical issues, including sustainable food. It throws parties. It celebrates the Fourth of July as well as Martin Luther King's and Gandhi's birthdays. It wants people to have fun. These and other practices became part of the secret sauce underlying White Dog Café's popularity.

Then, Judy gave all the secrets away. She started a non-profit foundation to teach her competitors about the importance of locally farmed products. She shared her suppliers. She invited her "rivals" to join her as part of the larger, sustainable, local food *system* she dreamt of.

She paid forward the lessons she had learned, and shared the opportunities she had cultivated. She recognized that her approach to business could be imitated by others, even other restaurants; and trained them to do so. This, she knew, would benefit the entire "food shed."

Judy Wicks and the White Dog Café act with reciprocity. We can act with reciprocity ourselves — to support those organizations that support us. Our decisions about where we shop, where we bank, which charities we support, where we invest — each is a decision about how to use "the money tool." When we consider others' needs alongside our own, we are using it with a sense of reciprocity.

Takeaways from this chapter

Generosity is an antidote to business, which sees outcomes only in terms of its own, immediate self-interest. Generosity or reciprocity (by which I mean giving without conditions) can guide us. We can think about using our resources in ways that go beyond only helping ourselves. (Businesses can, too.)

SPEND INTO THE FUTURE

Our home

On the Fourth of July, 2019, a heat dome trapped hot air over Alaska, pushing temperatures in Anchorage to 90°F (32°C) , an all-time high.[6] The following June, a heatwave in Siberia pushed temperatures above 100°F. CNN ran a story with the headline "Are parts of India becoming too hot for humans?"[7] Most frighteningly, the average temperature of the planet has risen to a level that no human life has ever known.[8]

Yet, often without much thought, we all buy and use products or services that contribute to this problem: cars, air travel, food, or goods transported from other continents. The climate is on fire because of us — because of how we, as a society, make things and ship things, plus our insatiable desires, and habits, as consumers.

On the same Independence Day, there were about 150 incidents of gun violence in the United States, resulting in

40 deaths, including 10 children or teens, plus 77 injuries. There was probably a mass shooting somewhere. This is what occurs every day in this country, where businesses can legally sell weapons designed for war. In a very unfortunate sense, we are a land of equal opportunity: a majority of adults say they, or someone they care for, has experienced gun violence.[9]

We shop at Bass Pro Shops (one of the country's largest privately owned companies) and its subsidiary, Cabela's. Although we don't buy guns there, they do sell them, including military-style weapons like the semi-automatic AR-15 which has been used in numerous mass killings. And they continue to sell them, even in the wake of appalling murders such as the one at Marjory Stoneman Douglas High School in Parkland, Florida, on Valentine's Day 2018, which killed 14 students and three others. The AR-15, to many, is "America's Rifle."

We get what we pay for.

If corporations are complicit in profiting from climate-destroying products and weapons, then so are we: we buy from them. If we spent differently, we can hope they would take notice and change their behavior. If we spent differently, maybe cars, trucks, and planes would become radically more fuel-efficient, helping us head off the very worst effects of the climate crisis. If we spent differently, maybe companies would stop selling assault rifles, thus preventing many cruel and pointless deaths. If we spent differently, maybe more of the local businesses nearby would survive. Maybe more people would be employed. Maybe our communities would feel less hollowed out.

And, if we continue to spend as we are, we signal our acceptance of the things around us.

We are spenders

Money will *not* solve all of our problems. But it can help solve some, so it's useful to know where the money is. Here are some ballpark figures:

Source	Amount ($ billions)
Foreign aid (world)	142
Charity (U.S.)	390
GDP (spending) (world)	84,000

These numbers are hard to comprehend. Who has ever had a billion of anything, let alone a trillion? (GDP is $84 trillion.) However, it's easy to compare sizes: for every $100 of foreign assistance given around the world, there is $275 of charitable giving (that's just in the U.S., but we contribute the most to charity by far), and almost $60,000 of spending.

Spending provides a gigantic lever for change.

The average U.S. household spends about 80–90% of what its earners bring home. Most is spent on housing, food, and transportation — some of our basic needs. There are differences among us, of course: if you're wealthy, you own; if you're not, you rent. Some of us dine out more (certainly pre-Covid). We all spend about the same percentage on transportation, but that includes everything from paying for bus fare to buying a Mercedes. As a society, between two-thirds and three-quarters of our spending is on basic needs.

How we spend makes a difference in terms of the good (or bad) we do in so many ways. To add to the examples I highlighted before, how our food is grown can be destructive or supportive of the environment; where we buy our clothes can contribute to sweatshops or to workers receiving fairer wages and safer working conditions; and, to emphasize again, our choices about transportation add up to huge differences in the quality of the air and the temperature of the planet.

Poll after poll shows we would like our purchasing to do good. But it's hard, and often we don't make those better choices.

One overwhelming reason is it can very often cost more. We'd prefer a pair of "socially beneficial" socks, but we end up buying ones that are less expensive. We try on something locally, then find our size on Amazon, where it's cheaper (and which quashes our impulse to do good by being so convenient).

It also takes effort to figure out how "socially beneficial" (or harmful) something really is. Quite often we act with willful ignorance, too — by which I mean we won't make the effort to explore the societal effects of what we buy even if we suspect there are more societally friendly choices to be made. (To make ourselves feel better about that, we may even denigrate those who actually *do* make the effort and *do* re-direct their spending.[10])

But buying with greater intention is a key component of doing good with money. It may not be easy but it is powerful. There are literally trillions of dollars of consumer spending on the table. There is information out there that can help us, but, before we explore it, let us first acknowledge something — a half-trillion-dollar beast — that makes it so hard to make good choices. I'm talking about advertising.

May we grab your attention

We may say we buy mostly for practical reasons, but researchers know this is not true. Buying things, online or in stores, serves many ends: diversion, sensory stimulation, creating community, signaling status.[11] In fact, most of us recognize this at least at some level. Advertisers certainly do: they grab our attention; they don't politely request it. They're powerful enough to make us need things we don't want and throw our doing-good-with-money intentions completely out the window.

Coca-Cola was originally a patent medicine containing tiny amounts of cocaine. Now it seems more likely to cause disease than cure it. The Coca-Cola Company, worth more than $200 billion as I write, today offers hundreds of different beverages, not just its famous soft drink. It also spends more than $4 billion a year getting us to drink them. Pepsico, the parent company of Pepsi-Cola, created an advertising campaign which classified its products as "Good for You," "Better for You [than its alternatives]," or "Fun for You" — the latter a euphemism for containing lots of sugar, salt, or fat. Pepsico, as Coke's younger sibling, spends "only" $2.5 billion a year on advertising.

DeBeers, a South African company, went as far as to make diamond engagement rings "Necessary for You." DeBeers was formed by combining the financial and mining interests of the diamond industry to create the world's largest cartel. It controlled the mining of diamonds in Southern Africa for more than a century, and could make diamonds valuable by keeping them scarce. But DeBeers still had to make people want them.

Around the start of World War II, diamond prices had plummeted, and DeBeers badly needed help. They contacted an American advertising firm, N.W. Ayer, to see if "the use of *propaganda* [my italics] in various forms" might be useful.[12] A close relationship followed, which lasted several decades.

A basic strategy was formulated for boosting sales and keeping prices high.[13]

First, you make both bride and groom feel inadequate unless there was a diamond engagement ring in the picture. You hammer home the equation "diamond rings = romance." Ad campaigns traded on the status of movie stars and other high-society figures, even Queen Elizabeth. Second, you discourage women from ever reselling their rings. Fearing that the public owned fifty times the number of diamonds that De Beers could mine in a year (and that a vigorous second-hand market would therefore pose a massive threat), in 1948 DeBeers adopted the slogan "A Diamond Is Forever," which has been seen on all DeBeers' advertisements since. The reselling of a ring came to mean violating a taboo. In 1999, *Advertising Age* named "A Diamond is Forever" the slogan of the century.

The propaganda has worked. In the United States, the percentage of brides receiving diamond engagement rings rose from 10% in 1939 to 80% in 1990.[14] The advertising was just as effective in Japan, effecting a change from a 1,500-year-old tradition of drinking rice wine from wooden bowls (to signify marriage) to receiving a diamond ring (to show you're engaged). In 1955, fewer than 5% of Japanese woman received a diamond engagement ring, but now the figure is just a shade below the United States.[15] More recently, China has discovered this same "need" for diamond rings, and is satisfying it more quickly.

So, for one thing, let's not pretend we are always mindful shoppers. For another thing, the enemy knows what it's doing. Coke is sugar water, diamonds are carbon molecules that have been compressed underground. The former is associated with diabetes; the latter with warlords, insurgencies, and forced labor. But their success in the marketplace has been exquisitely engineered.

Can we fight back? Can we find products and services with "virtuous" features? Can we support businesses where wellbeing is woven in through and through — where employees, communities, and the planet as a whole are well served? Unless we can tell the difference between companies that protect the planet and those that destroy it — or those who uphold labor rights and those who trample them — it's impossible to make a buying decision based on such criteria. But, when we do know, we have a choice.

So we must be armed — with information.

Labels, as a start: what *is* that product?

Labels are everywhere. We can read the labels, and we ought to. But things can get confusing, and fast. If you think eggs are best described as either scrambled, fried, or over-easy, you've not been paying much attention to labels.

USDA-certified organic eggs are pesticide- and antibiotic-free, keeping those chemicals out of your body. *Omega-3 enriched* eggs come from chickens fed enhanced diets so that their eggs contain 100–600 mg of the heart-healthy Omega-3 that you want in your body. *Vegetarian-fed* eggs come from chickens fed a vegetarian diet without supplements or additives — and never, ever bacon. *Non-GMO* eggs may be more healthful than other eggs, but some people say they're not; but they sound like they are, and they serve the needs of consumers wanting to eat "natural."

And if your concern is with the environment?

Modern egg farms are considerably more efficient than they were in the past because they use less water, less feed, and produce fewer greenhouse gases. But these efficiencies can come at the expense of the chickens themselves, who are often looked at as nothing more than dispensable components of an egg factory. Are there labels, then, to describe how well the chickens are treated?

Several good-sounding labels actually lead to more confusion. *Organic* egg farming means chickens must have some cage-free, outdoor access — but it may not be much. The *United Egg Producer* certified egg label means there was a third-party audit to ensure that hens are well treated. But *free-range* and *pasture-raised* are labels that can be earned without an audit, meaning they may be only marketing-friendly. Higher up the ethical food chain are *certified humane* eggs (for which the starving or stressing of hens [practices leading to larger eggs] are banned, although beak-cutting is still allowed). Highest of all, we find *animal welfare approved* eggs (audited, no beak-cutting, no starving or stressing, and no chicks thrown into chippers [really, this happens — sorry to be the one to tell you]).

And all of the above is just eggs and their labels. Yes, labels can be useful. But if we pay that much attention to all the food we buy, how will we ever make it through a supermarket? We'd be overwhelmed. And there are still clothes to buy, and books, and furniture, and cars and . . . all with their own set of concerns. How can we possibly shop in ways that align with our values?

(Remember here — and as you continue to read — the comforting notion of a 15% solution.)

Apps to help us sort

As this book was being completed, GoodGuide announced that, after 13 years, it was "taking a break" having served over 10 million customers and explored half a million products.[16] Its stated aim was to educate "consumers to make better choices . . . to drive the development of safer, healthier, and more sustainable products." GoodGuide is — now *was* — an app for helping consumers find products aligned with their values. Originally the app (and website) evaluated a wide variety of products on a number of pro-societal dimensions, from labor conditions to the environment to personal health. More recently, GoodGuide focused solely on personal care, certain household chemicals, and products for babies and children. Even then, it evaluated over 75,000 products on 14 categories for serious health hazards, relying on scientific information to examine products' ingredients. It scored ingredients according to their potential hazards. Users could see both the score and the level of completeness of the underlying data.

I wish GoodGuide would return from its break; we need credible information. I admired what I appreciated as an accurate, scientific approach behind its product recommendations. And, at least initially, it provided information about a huge number of different products. It made a promise to inform us, not sell to us. It pulled together facts to help us make choices.

Even so, as you are reading this, there are apps to help us shop and "do good": supporting workers' rights, protecting the planet, avoiding waste. None is comprehensive; some rate only one thing: for example, seafood.

Finding an app will usually be a lot easier than finding information *about* the app. Many don't tell you *how* they calculate their ratings; and they may not be as rigorous as you would require. As a rule of thumb: if an organization has enjoyed a good reputation in a particular area even before it issued an app, then the ratings its app produces might be more trustworthy. Always do your homework when choosing an app!

Some potentially helpful apps available at time of publication are listed and described in Appendix 1.

Listen to barking watchdogs: understanding companies and industries

Watchdog agencies typically focus on one particular issue and follow it for years. Acting as our eyes and ears, they alert us to what's going on and can spur us into action. Watchdogs have full-time staff and subject-area expertise, including local knowledge. When they investigate companies or industries, they do so in depth and with rigor; when they report their results, they usually spell out their methodology so we understand the basis for their conclusions and recommendations.

As an example: since the late 1990s Amazon Watch has been monitoring developments in the Amazon rainforest, trying both to protect this vital biome for the health of the planet and to protect and defend indigenous people who've lived there for centuries but whose land (and way of life) is now being overrun by modern business. Its website states its priorities: stopping the destruction of the Amazon; letting indigenous people participate in the development of solutions that affect them concerning climate change, natural resource extraction, or industrial development; and supporting climate justice.

Amazon Watch produces well-researched reports on these issues. Recent reports implicate major businesses around the world that are destroying the Amazon for commercial gain, as well as the major banking and financial firms that provide them with their funding.[17] The connections between businesses and the destruction of the Amazon are covered in Chapter 9, "Investing for Real Impact."

Later in this chapter, we'll discuss two other watchdog agencies: the Institute of Public & Environmental Affairs, a Chinese watchdog that monitors and helps reduce pollution from Chinese factories; and Human Rights Watch, which protects and advocates on behalf of vulnerable groups by investigating and reporting on issues like migrant camps, treatment of refugees, and workers' rights.

Like Amazon Watch, these watchdogs have a deep, nuanced, and practical understanding of the problem they're involved with and the region of the world they cover. They rely on a combination of local knowledge and specialized skills. With paid, professional staff, watchdogs produce well-researched reports that show us how our actions at home relate to social or environmental outcomes we care about around the globe; and the effects of which can keep bad behavior (child labor, as a ready example) in check. Watchdogs' reports about companies and industries can help you make informed choices around issues you care about.

Then there are websites that also offer recommendations about products and companies, but which employ a less rigorous approach in their evaluations and are less forthcoming about their methods. As with apps, relying on websites with a track record of providing credible information is a good rule of thumb.

Both watchdogs and a few of the less rigorous organizations can guide our purchasing on a gamut of societal issues. A sample of these organizations is listed in Appendix 2. Again, choosing one area where you can do good with your spending is fine: you don't need to do everything. There is a likely a watchdog barking just for you.

A new breed of companies: pick the *companies* you want to buy from

A new breed of companies is rising, carrying the B Corp banner. It's a banner that stands for environmentally sustainable and societally responsible companies. A banner we should get behind.

So what is a B Corp? Since 2006, the B Corp movement has been working with for-profit businesses, with an ambition to define, measure, transform, and support businesses desiring to do societal good. B Corps commit to more than just profit.

Certifying bodies have long served social purposes, making sure our products are safe, our buildings are green, and our Pilates instructors have at least a minimal idea what they're doing. B Corp certification shows us which businesses place a commitment to doing good at their very core.

B Lab offers B Corp certification. Its website proclaims:

- Vote Every Day.
- Vote B Corp.
- You cast your vote every day with the choices you make — what you buy, where you work and who you do business with.

- You have the power to make your voice heard beyond the ballot box.
- Every day is election day.

The following are some highlights of B Lab's electioneering.

B Lab is a non-profit, but it helps for-profit businesses assess their social and environmental performance, become better corporate citizens, and display their commitment to "doing good" (for the world).

B Lab's free assessment tool, B Impact Assessment, gathers information about companies' impact on workers, the community, and the environment, and about their governance. For example, three (out of many) questions about a company's environmental impact — from the B Impact Assessment website[18] — are:

- What % of energy (relative to company revenues) was saved in the last year for your corporate facilities?
- Does your company monitor and record its universal waste production?
- Which is the broadest community with whom your environmental reviews/audits are formally shared?

From its answers, a company is scored on different facets of its environmental impact — everything from the inputs it uses and the products (or services) it produces, to its office and land, its emissions, waste, transportation, and even the behavior of its suppliers. In all areas, it is compared to other businesses and finally given an overall environmental score. It is assessed separately on its impact on workers, on the communities where it operates, and on its internal governance. Another set of B Lab tools helps companies take steps to improve in any impact area.

Companies that score high enough on their overall impact assessment can then become a certified B Corporation — or a B Corp, as they are more popularly known. But first they must agree to an audit and a tour of their facilities. And then they must adopt one of several legal forms — often a *benefit corporation* in the United States.

B Corp certification means a company is acting as a good corporate citizen, but it is not a guarantee that it always will. Companies can choose various forms of legal registration, and the vast majority choose one that allows them to exclusively pursue their own self-interest (as long as they stay within the law). B Corp certification requires companies to legally commit *not* to place *stock*holders' interests above those of other *stake*holders (workers, the local community) or the environment. This legally protects a company's societal mission if someone tries to buy it, new leaders are brought in, or when it seeks money from new investors who might have different ideas about making a profit. After paying its dues and agreeing to periodic, ongoing audits, a company can display the B Corp symbol.

B Corps are companies where employees want to work, whose communities want them there, and whose environmental practices are commendable. They are companies from whom we should want to buy. Danone North America is a B Corp — the world's largest — and displays the B Corp symbol on its homepage. Seventh Generation, the company devoted to environmental sustainability in its cleaning products, displays the B Corp symbol directly on the products it sells. But identifying B Corp companies isn't as easy as it should be.

One of Danone North America's brands is Horizon Organic. But the B Corp symbol is not to be seen either on its Horizon Organic sour cream nor on its Wallaby Organic yogurt. Ben & Jerry's lets the world know its packaging is environmentally friendly by placing the FSC checkmark tree on its ice cream carton, which also boasts that its ingredients are non-GMO. But nowhere does the B Corp symbol appear, even though Ben & Jerry's has earned the right to display it.

So how can consumers know which products are made by B Corp certified companies? At the moment, the question is challenging. For now, the best answer is to do the research beforehand, so you can shop with your values. Here, the Certified B Corp directory[19] will help you.

B Corps are a relatively new phenomenon, unknown to most of us. Larger companies may still be reluctant to position themselves as "do good companies," possibly wary of alienating mainstream customers. Small companies, which comprise 90% of all B Corps, may not have the marketing skills nor the budget to promote their membership of the B Corp community. But two-thirds of us are willing to pay more for sustainable products,[20] so it seems likely that B Corps will increasingly come to wear their status on their corporate sleeves. And more companies will become B Corps, including major companies. But, for now, at the time of writing there are still over 2,500 B Corps to look for.

Do *we* make a difference?

Ma Jun, once a Chinese journalist, founded a non-profit organization to bring attention to and address the pollution caused by Chinese manufacturing. In 2013, China suffered an "Airpocalypse," when fine particulate matter in Beijing averaged nine times the level the World Health Organization deemed safe, at times spiking to 30–45 times that much; in other parts of China, the problem was up to 50% worse.

The national government instituted laws requiring all manufacturing plants to report, in real time, the level of their emissions. A good step, but not enough to change their behavior. For starters, the government remained as concerned as ever about the economy, and violating companies often simply got their wrists slapped or could bribe their way out of a penalty. So if laws and fines couldn't change their behavior, what could?

The Institute of Public & Environmental Affairs (IPE),[21] the non-profit watchdog that Ma Jun founded, took steps that were both agreeable to the government and effective in getting companies to (literally) clean up their act. First, it created the China Air Pollution Map, an app to display the same real-time data the government was mandating businesses to report. If you were walking past a factory belching smoke, you no longer had to guess how bad its pollution was: your phone could tell you.

But who were these factories producing *for*? Typically, multinational companies headquartered in the U.S. and other parts of the developed world. Perhaps *they* could be pressured into making a difference? So IPE augmented its map with the brand names associated with the factory emissions. IPE wanted the remote downstream companies to acknowledge China's factory pollution as their own.

❖ ❖ ❖

In 2012, fires destroyed garment factories in Bangladesh and Pakistan. The following year the Rana Plaza factory building in Bangladesh collapsed. The deaths of 1,400 workers from these events, and serious injuries to over 2,000 others, were traced to unsound buildings, unsafe working conditions, inadequate safety procedures, and coercive labor practices. The workers were among the lowest-paid in the world.

At the time of these tragedies, global manufacturing companies were able to deny any connection to these factories because they had hired middlemen agencies to contract with the factories on their behalf, thereby shielding them from direct knowledge — and hence complicity — about where their goods were being made. Though the United States has regulations in place to help prevent similar tragedies at home, American companies seek low-wage countries with few (or no) regulations as cheap manufacturing sites. What they can't get away with at home, they take overseas.

❖ ❖ ❖

IPE took an additional, and vital, step to play on companies' sensitivity about their public image. When a factory owned by Zhejiang Saintyear Textile Co., one of China's biggest manufacturing companies, was out of compliance, IPE contacted its largest customers, such as Wal-Mart, Nike, Gap, and H&M. IPE listed the violations and convinced these companies not to place orders with Saintyear (or any other violating suppliers) until these global brands' *own* professed environmental standards were met by the Saintyear factory. In one fell swoop, IPE transferred the responsibility for emissions problems from Chinese factories back to developed-world companies.

IPE also produces an annual transparency index,[22] which ranks and scores nearly 500 brands on how well they monitor and insist on improvements in the factories in which their products are made. According to a recent report, the best environmental stewards are Dell, Levi's, and the Belgian-Dutch-German retailer C&A; far, far below them in the rankings are companies such as Hello Bike and LOCK &

LOCK (a South Korean household products company) along with better-known names like NIVEA, DKNY, and Facebook. Taken as a whole, transparency scores are rising year on year.

❖ ❖ ❖

Five years after the tragedies in garment factories in Bangladesh and Pakistan, the international non-profit Human Rights Watch examined the transparency of global apparel companies.[23] Its report, "Follow the Thread," describes the responses of 72 global apparel companies one year after they were asked to make a pledge to disclose publicly the whereabouts of their factories and the conditions within those factories. The report shows that fewer than one-third of these companies agreed both to make the pledge and to produce goods only in safety-compliant factories.

"Follow the Thread" finds Levi's, Nike, and Patagonia to be the most transparent about their factories and sees them taking steps to improve them. American Eagle, Wal-Mart, and other companies, however, refused even to commit to being transparent about which factories their goods were made in.

Human Rights Watched observed:

> When global supply chains are opaque, consumers often lack meaningful information about where their apparel was made. A T-shirt label might say "Made in China," but in which of the country's thousands of factories was this garment made? And under what conditions for workers?

❖ ❖ ❖

Watchdogs shine a light on bad corporate behavior; sometimes they create publicity that is embarrassing enough to cause corporations to change. We are free to dig into these reports ourselves and use the information to guide our purchasing (and there are other tools at our disposal). We, too, can cause corporations to take notice and change their behavior.

Live in the future

If we desire a well-functioning society — and if to achieve this we see change as being urgent, moral, or necessary — we must live mindfully: in the future. Make it ours before it gets here. Live (and buy) with reciprocity. Recognize how we might spread our good fortune. Choose our products, and the companies who make them, with care.

Living in the future means imagining the way you want things to be; and believing in that future by acting to make it so.

Takeaways from this chapter

We all spend most of what we earn. Which means: if we want to do good with money, our spending is a great place to start. Be more conscious about consumption. Know where your money goes — who uses it, and whether they're using it well or abusing the privilege. Recognize that businesses are producing too much for the planet to sustain us: buy less. Avoid products (and companies) that cause harm.

4 STAY HOME

Local businesses help communities thrive by providing economic and civic advantages. They anchor communities and lend their personalities.

But local businesses can do something else: they can create a sense of connection. In perhaps subtle — but important — ways, this can encourage us to think of exchange as something kinder, and more generous: an attitude that we might then bring to all our relationships.

This chapter explores these two issues: first, the tangible economic and social benefits that local businesses provide; and, second, the idea that local businesses may induce a sense of caring and connection that otherwise is absent when we buy things without considering relationships.

The economic and civic benefits of local business

The next few sections will describe local businesses in economic and civic terms. Highlights among the conclusions are that local businesses make good neighbors; that they are excellent job creators; and they inculcate a strong sense of civic responsibility and connection. But, before diving into that, I will allow a little space for a focus on big business, where we'll see how their success is often at the expense of communities.

Bigger ≠ better

Since the end of World War II, the United States and much of the world has grown increasingly used to, and enamored of, big business.

Immediately after the war, this was understandable. The country found itself with an industrial base raring to churn out products at high volume, and consumers hungry to buy them. Big business could serve a need in the wake of so much sacrifice. In the decades that followed, and spurred by the rise of an increasingly global economy, "bigger (and more efficient) is better" became a self-evident "truth."

But the real truth is different.

You may have seen stories like this one from Oxfam, the world-renowned organization working for economic equality and inclusion:[24] 2,153 billionaires in the world have more combined wealth than the poorest 4.6 billion people. Put a little differently, each billionaire has, on average, more wealth than the combined assets of 2.1 million people. Many of these super-rich are in technology-related fields, where huge successful bets have been placed on speed, convenience, and scale. Others are in finance, the recipients of ludicrously large returns on their gambles. For them, economics is a powerful force, one that continuously churns out new products and seduces consumers into buying them, thereby generating an ever-increasing national wealth.

But, on the other end of the economic spectrum, times are very tough. Income inequality in the United States has risen almost every year in the last 50, and now is at its highest point ever.[25] Covid has exposed how clock-punching employees are often viewed as dispensable and replaceable — assets, not people. Companies worth billions can even maneuver to avoid providing them with benefits such as health insurance.

Is this how we want wealth to be shared?

Also, big businesses often behave more like itinerant visitors than neighbors — just passing through on their way elsewhere. The Wal-Mart near you is probably nothing more than a row on a spreadsheet to an accountant in Bentonville, Arkansas (where Wal-Mart has its headquarters). When the numbers are looking bad, there's always a more attractive location than yours. But, by the time it has packed up and left, that Wal-Mart has driven out smaller, local businesses, which have shut their doors forever.

The effects of these big businesses are felt beyond the workplace. Some will bargain with the communities into which they plan to move, insisting on this tax advantage or that change in zoning. When cities or towns inattentively (or reluctantly) agree to these stipulations, they are often inflicting on their neighborhoods such a huge level of change (single family homes being supplanted by more luxurious apartment buildings, for example) that long-time residents can no longer afford to live there, or else they see their favorite shops and restaurants make way for those that cater to the new residents. Businesses shape the communities we live in.

Small businesses are different. Being small, they can't take over a town; they fit in. And because they are, with *very* few exceptions, owned and operated locally, they stay put. And they don't leave an unfillable vacuum if they do close their doors.

We like local businesses; we like them a lot and we prefer to shop locally. In fact, 92% of us have a favorable view of locally owned and controlled businesses[26] —far more positive than how we feel about our major corporations. Most of us find fault with major companies when it comes to how they (fail to) support local communities, protect the environment, and create jobs. American's confidence in big business has been close to rock bottom for nearly two decades, while confidence in small business hovers near 70%.[27]

Yet large businesses bask in the glow of inevitable progress. Small businesses — which is another way of saying local businesses — harken back to simpler times when business seemed cozy and not necessarily efficient.

So, even if we find aspects of big business distasteful, we're still left wondering: aren't big businesses the engine that drives us forward? Hasn't the sun already set on small businesses — even if we like them? The answer is: no.

Creating jobs

Small (local) businesses are major job creators — and this is true under every definition of the term "small business." It may surprise you to learn that small businesses provide about half of all jobs in the United States, and generated about two-thirds of all job growth the last decade.[28] Startups provided about 30% of overall growth — which means that nearly 40% of job growth came from small firms other than startups. Young businesses that make it past infancy are among the most important job generators. Small businesses attract new businesses, thereby keeping a community growing. A community with many small, local businesses will create more jobs than one with fewer, larger businesses.[29] This benefits the entire county: job growth rises and the poverty rate falls.[30]

Nonetheless, small businesses are financially fragile, typically having only enough cash in the bank to stay open for several weeks if their customers vanish. If ever we needed proof that our spending is the lifeblood of local businesses, Covid provided it.

The economics of local

Communities dotted with small businesses are more tightly bound economically than communities dominated by large business. What happens when a Wal-Mart, for instance, enters a community?[31] Mom-and-pop retailers go out of business. But so might many others who support them: from lawyers, accountants, and advertising firms, to warehousing, logistics, and trucking companies. After all, Main Street talent will be unknown in Bentonville, Mumbai, or Shanghai: all of these locations have immense talent pools which can be leveraged to provide the services they need. When local establishments are put out of business, their founders may pack their bags to start over elsewhere. And with them they take another thread out of the community tapestry.

Where small businesses are the dominant feature of an economy, we can see something else in play. They form a resilient economic network: the local hardware store uses a local printer to produce its flyers; the printer uses a local accounting firm; and so on in ways that are economically reinforcing.

A study of ten communities found that, on average, 48% of the revenue accruing to local, independent businesses was ultimately re-spent within the community.[32] Another way to think of that is that every dollar spent at a local business generates almost another 50 cents in local spending. Chain stores in the same towns — like Barnes & Noble or Home Depot —spend much of their revenue outside the local community, depriving it of that extra investment. But, when money re-circulates, we see businesses buying supplies from other local companies, and people spending their wages in local shops and restaurants.

Appendix 3 provides concrete examples of how we can preserve, support, and extend local businesses. It covers "buy local" efforts, to help fend off the encroachment of non-local businesses, as well as suggestions for eating out and supporting sustainable agriculture.

Creating a civil culture

One problem is that local businesses can seem to fall short when measured against larger businesses. They pay somewhat less, and the very smallest pay the least. The jobs are less glamorous, too: more jobs in service and hospitality, and fewer jobs in IT and finance.

But, ever since large corporations began gaining economic clout and consolidating themselves within the economic landscape, critics have noted that they have rarely made good neighbors. This was true of communities dependent on coal mining, steel production, and automobile manufacturing in the days before the information and telecommunications revolution, when huge corporate profits didn't prevent frequent layoffs.[33] So it still is today: "good for the company" does not translate to "good for society." But reliable studies repeatedly show that small, local businesses do, in contrast, make good neighbors: they improve community life. They can be counted on to make their communities better. Let's look at some of the ways.

In localities free from domination by big businesses, people vote more, including in local elections.[34] Voter participation is recognized as an important indicator of community involvement: people feel their voice means something and that they will be heard. Participation is high because people are concerned about their community's best interests. Money for a new soccer field or improvements to the local library may seem nothing more than a financial burden to a company without local roots, but it means a better place to live for those who call that community their home.

Communities characterized by a network of small businesses enjoy many other benefits of civic engagement. Their children attend after-school activities — music, art, science, scouting. They play soccer on the fields their parents voted for. Education is better. More people live in homes that they own. Even incomes can be higher. Local businessmen and -women have a strong sense of their community's needs and serve in charitable, civic, and governmental roles to meet them. Major corporations want profitable stores, not vibrant communities. Ask yourself: do you tend to strike up a conversation at Wal-Mart? It's far more likely you do so at your favorite local coffee shop, your farmers' market, or your food co-op. Locally owned businesses are much more generous than national chain stores in contributing to local causes, including schools and local charities.[35] Communities with a concentration of small businesses exude an entrepreneurial culture. Small businesses generate 13 times as many patents per employee as larger businesses.[36] Research shows that the members of these communities are physically healthier, too (even when other economic factors are taken into account).[37]

Local business and local relationships

We've just seen some of the tangible benefits of local businesses. In summary:

- They are viewed more favorably than larger businesses.

- They are better job creators and better at attracting new business.

- They re-circulate money better than big businesses.

- They are associated with a strong civic culture, through higher rates of both homeownership and voting.

And, at an emotional level, they tap into something we value. Consider that, in the last few decades, local bookstores have had to face competition from bookstore chains in malls, the rise of Barnes & Noble and Borders (remember them?), then Amazon, and more recently the Kindle. Yet the number of local bookstores is now growing (though it is below the high-water mark of a few decades ago). How can this be? It is because local bookstores evoke the armchair not the drone; a human's taste not an algorithm's. Bookstores often serve as the anchor institution for "buy local" movements. They provide a gathering place where you might attend a lecture or a book signing, grab some coffee, or simply happen upon an interesting book. Humans like those things.

An even stronger statement about local businesses' value might be that they have made the commitment to *be* local. They've made a *choice* to be here: maybe they're a third-generation shoe store; or maybe this is simply where they want to be. They have tied their fate to a community. Local businesses forge relationships — with and among community members, and with other local businesses. And, with every genuine relationship, no matter how seemingly inconsequential, we move toward a better understanding of each other, and the possibility of a kinder, more respectful world. And this is what local businesses are contributing towards.

Money — physical or otherwise — is impersonal, and that often confuses us into thinking that all transactions must be that way, that it's fanciful to imagine money (or business) as anything but nameless and faceless. But, when relationships are involved, things change.

Most of us, in fact, already deal with exchange in personal ways. Within families, money doesn't change hands: I don't get paid if I wash the dishes; my daughters don't get paid when they help me with my computer. It's in the family, and we each do our bit. As a family, our ongoing relationship makes buying and selling from each other unnecessary; the very idea seems silly.

Giving gifts

Gift-giving has the same flavor. When you give a gift, you don't expect repayment. Giving a gift can say you care; it may express your kindness or generosity. Gifts help build relationships, back and forth. Those in enduring relationships will ultimately share both roles, giver and receiver.

This quote, which shows how permeable the boundary is between giving and receiving, is, to me, profound: "I never feel so given to as when you take from me." When you genuinely receive what I offer, I receive your appreciation or understanding in return; and when we are receivers, we can express (give the giver) that appreciation. With every gift, given and received, a relationship grows.

What is a gift? It can take any form: a material thing, of course; sometimes money. But we can also give the gift of our time, our attention, our consideration, our compassion, our labor . . . and whatever else we wish to share. When we pay attention to *these* currencies (forms of value), we realize we have more to spend (give/share) then we ever imagined. We can be wealthy in ways beyond money.

Gift-giving would appear to have nothing to do with economics. But, in fact, that is how many indigenous communities used to interact.[38] Often, there was no straight-up trading, only gift-giving. If you gave me something I needed, at some point you might remind me, and I'd give you what you needed if I had it. And so a web of relationships arose, individual needs linked in communal interest. Those on the receiving end of a gift would look forward to some day returning the favor, grateful for the security of a community that supported them and the opportunity to strengthen it by giving back. In certain societies, a special gift might even be given to signify that giver and receiver — as well as their families — had entered a relationship of mutual obligation, where they would contribute to each other's material well-being for the *rest of their lives*.[39] Economies based on gifting and sharing show us that the way we usually "do business" is not the only way.

Connected by money

Local businesses, as we have seen, are means by which relationships are fostered. What's more, they can do business in ways in which they are truly *giving*. White Dog Café, as you'll recall, cultivates relationships — with everyone from employees to customers, suppliers, and even competitors. It wants them all to thrive and looks for ways to support them, forming a web of mutual support. It reminds us that we can come together, rather than solely looking out for our own interests.

As White Dog Café's founder Judy Wicks explains, proprietors once lived above their stores; so when they went downstairs to work, they simply brought their "upstairs" values down with them.[40] But when people began to work for others, outside their homes, things changed: employees were expected to leave their personal values at home and adopt those of the company. As the only corporate "value" destined to prevail was the pursuit of profit, this motive was expected to govern the behavior of everyone under the company's roof. You could always quit your job, but you were there to hire out your labor, not provide an opinion on civics or morality.

Yet the core values of its founder remain embedded in White Dog Café: togetherness, resilience, and justice. This small business demonstrates that we can treat people as people (not simply customers or employees); we can treat them with respect and honesty; and provide for the common welfare.

I once took a five-mile drive sitting in the passenger seat of my car so my mechanic could drive my car himself to listen for the noise I was trying to describe. When we got back, he said nothing was really the matter and told me, "No charge." He is honest, trustworthy, and looks out for what's in my best interest, not just his own. I know this because I've dealt with him over such a long time. I'm not just getting my car fixed, I'm getting it fixed by someone with whom I have a relationship and who I trust won't fix things that don't need fixing. And this works in the other direction: he knows me as a long-time, returning customer with trust in his shop. I don't know how many family cars my mechanic has serviced over the years but between my wife, my kids, and me it's a lot. Helping me like he did was an unexpected surprise, which meant something to me and which I accepted with appreciation. For my part, even though I know a new battery will cost more at his place than others, I will gladly pay it.

In the mechanic's shop there are posters on the wall that imply that the mechanic and I diverge in our political values and beliefs. But relationships can help us see beyond differences and look for common ground. This understanding, in turn, makes it more likely we might work together, rather than against each other, in more clearly seeing and addressing societal issues.

I used to get coffee at a small shop up the highway a few times a year. I'd stop in, buy coffee, put in some half-and-half, spend some time chatting with the owner, and be gone. I never learned his name, but over the years I knew his age, I knew about his stint with the Marines, and how war chemicals had ruined his health. I asked about him when he wasn't there. I knew about some of his battles with insurance companies and his life-saving surgeries. Over many conversations, we'd developed a relationship. The last time I saw him, he told me he was retiring, just as I was. He wanted to spend more time outside, on the water, sitting on a small lake in a small boat. I liked learning that about him best of all. I felt a fondness for that coffee shop owner, a scrappy entrepreneur with a good heart. I hoped for his success in a way I would never feel about a Starbucks.

Maybe these are little things, but they break the mold of thinking profit is the only way for business to keep score. They tell us that *time = money* is not the only equation to describe how we interact with people. When someone feels like your neighbor, you want to lend a hand, just as they will lend theirs to you. When a business is locally *owned*, the owner almost always works there. Which means we can actually get to know them. And, after a while, we may find we're no longer just exchanging money for goods. When a business is locally *controlled*, it may adapt itself to the community's needs. Maybe workers' needs for time off are accommodated when their kids are in a school play, they have doctors' appointments, or they just need to catch their breath. Maybe a shop chooses a local after-school program or a senior center to support with donations of its products or by offering its skills. Maybe a mechanic decides to take a drive with you to listen for a noise so he can serve you better. I can't imagine a major car dealership ever letting someone step away from doing repairs to take a ride with a customer.

Businesses can be attentive to relationships — relationships with their employees, their customers, their communities. They will continue to need to make money so they can keep their business going and provide for their staff and themselves. But that is not the only thing. They can be "paid" in ways that don't involve money.

Economists tell us that the earliest kind of economic exchange was barter — say trading one horse for two sheep — which pre-dated money. In bartering, both sides try to come out ahead. But anthropologists tell us that there is no evidence that communities that bartered ever actually existed! Sometimes, different "tribes" might encounter each other and trade goods. And those events were punctuated by mock hostility, emphasizing that neither side wanted any ongoing relationship with the other. But *within* a community (a "tribe"), where there were continuing relationships, there was trust, gifting, and reciprocity.[41] Eventually, gifts and reciprocity gave way to debt (IOUs). Money only came into being after that, when debts started to be recorded (among a few, familiar people, memory could be enough) and it became the "common denominator" for all debts. This made debts impersonal. You could now transfer a debt you were *owed by* Annie to pay off a *debt to* Zelda — which was not possible when debts were associated with one-to-one relationships.

After a while, money became completely de-linked from relationships. Money was just . . . money. Useful in any context, no connection to past gifts or exchange, able to be spent in any way one chose. Exchange no longer involved knowing someone; it had become impersonal. And from this our notion of business has evolved.

When we appreciate the importance of relationships, we do things that might sound odd to someone who sees "doing business" only in economic terms. For instance, some communities issue local currencies. These can be actual bills and coins that you carry in your wallet (such as BerkShares, used in the Berkshire region of Massachusetts[42]). But they can only be used at certain local stores — they're not as all-purpose as ordinary money; an economist would say they're less "useful." But people use local currencies to keep local businesses healthy and strong by re-circulating money among them. In a similar way, a $25 gift card to a bookstore can only be used there — but it's a gift connecting giver, recipient, and store, and so it is a more personal, memorable gift than the equivalent amount of cash.

These approaches make us feel *connected* through economics. It's an impulse that underlies timebanking. Under this system, an hour of a baker's time is worth an hour of an accountant's time or a tutor's time. When you do an hour of work, you bank that hour, and later you can withdraw it to pay for an hour of someone else's labor. Unlike money-based exchange, timebanking emphasizes what we have in common: no one's time is more valuable than anyone else's.

Perhaps it's a stretch to hope that every local business will always create all the benefits I've suggested. But, for too long now, we've stretched too far in the other direction — where money and business are simply conceived of as tools for exchange, as value-free as a hammer. For many of us, money "cues" us to become players in a competitive game, the idea of which is to accumulate, to press our advantage, and walk away ahead. But, as our examples show, money (or the will to forgo it) can also serve an alternative goal: helping us tame the desire to win at all costs, and instead to cultivate relationships that unite us.

It's been said that humans are the only species that would perish if there were no money. Money is merely a metaphor for how we interact with each other, but, because it touches so many aspects of our lives, we rarely, if ever, give this truth a moment's thought (we are like fish who do not see the water they are swimming in). But we can allow ourselves to take the opposite perspective: we can first notice how we want to interact with each other, and *then* envision how money can serve those ends. Money (and business) can thereby be harnessed to the purpose of supporting each other, rather than embodying a strategy for greatest individual gain.

My father lived in the same community his entire adult life. The last 20 years he was alive, he and a group of about eight friends got together every week for lunch. Always on a Thursday, same restaurant, same time, same table in the back — which the restaurant always held for them. One by one, members of the "Think Tank," as they called themselves, passed away. Each time, the restaurant hung a framed picture of this "family member" on the wall, honoring that life.

Takeaways from this chapter

Communities benefit when you spend money at local shops. It re-circulates, so every buck might create, say, $1.50–$2.00 of economic activity. Local purchasing allows local economies to stay alive and thrive. Buying local emphasizes relationships, which are key to economic, civic, and *personal* wellbeing.

5 A MEMO FROM ROBERT FROST

Twice in "Mending Wall," poet Robert Frost has his neighbor say, "Good fences make good neighbors." In the poem he takes issue with his neighbor's desire to maintain the boundary between them. How can *we* follow Frost's inclination to *include* our neighbors?

On a trip to Puerto Rico in 1946, an American woman, with no business experience, struck upon an idea that launched what we now call the fair trade movement. Seeing women in La Plata Valley who could make beautiful, embroidered textiles, but who were struggling to feed their families, Edna Ruth Byler realized that a heartfelt form of commerce might improve their lives. So she bought some of their pieces, paying them a fair price. When she returned home to Pennsylvania, she sold them to friends and neighbors. She spent the next three decades creating a marketplace for artisanal crafts produced by women like those she had met. In the early days, she'd stuff their goods into the trunk of her car, traveling across the country to talk about them and sell them — at sewing circles or whenever else she was welcomed into someone's home. By 1996, this effort had bloomed into the non-profit, fair trade retailer Ten Thousand Villages.

Ten Thousand Villages establishes long-term relationships with artisans (usually longer than a decade). Over the course of the relationship, Ten Thousand Villages works with artisans to identify products that will be appealing in Ten Thousand Villages' shops and then ensures that the prices the artisans receive are fair and sufficient for building their businesses and supporting their families. Twenty-one cents of each sales dollar goes to the artisans; in contrast, they would typically receive just a penny by selling through other retailers. There are other arrangements to benefit the artisans. Their long-term relationships with the store help them secure business loans. Ten Thousand Villages pays them one-half of what they are owed when an order is placed, which provides working capital, keeping them out of debt in the period before their goods sell. Equally importantly, Ten Thousand Villages buys items outright (rather than on consignment, or "sale or return"), further reducing artisans' risks.

Today, Ten Thousand Villages has about 70 stores in the United States (plus an online presence), with annual sales of over $25 million. Ten Thousand Villages has supported 20,000 artisans, the majority of them women, from 30 developing countries, providing over $140 million in income.

Beginning in the late 1980s, fair trade advocates sought to formalize support for small-scale farmers. Farmer co-operatives in developing countries had long been promoting fairer wages, workers' rights, and workplaces based on democratic governance; but now they would be connected to world markets. The idea was that coffee drinkers in the United States and Europe, where nearly 90% of the world's coffee is drunk, would pay a bit more to provide better support for marginalized workers half a world away. The higher price would provide several sources of economic support. Price floors would ensure that co-operative member-farmers would always receive enough for their coffee to at least cover their costs, even when market prices plummeted. Bonus payments (also called fair trade premiums or social premiums) would be paid to benefit farmers' communities or co-operatives. These premiums — now 20 cents per pound — might go toward schools, healthcare, water treatment, or improving productivity. Co-operatives' members vote on how to use these premiums.

Products grown and sold as fair trade were once found only in fair trade shops, but once coffee began to be certified and labeled *fair trade*, it could be sold anywhere, and the concept gained greater recognition. A series of fair trade labels followed, as well as international standards. Today, different strands of fair trade embrace different principles, but all agree on the necessity for stable, non-poverty incomes for famers, as well as sustainable agriculture. Other fair trade products now include bananas, cocoa, and cotton. Fair trade products are now grown in over 70 countries

Taking the farmer out of the coffee

A Starbucks Reserve Roastery assaults your senses. To one side you'll see a mixology bar, half caffeine, half alcohol, fuels to coax us up in the morning and settle us at night. Huge wooden beams cross the ceiling and silos filled with coffee beans line the walls. A gift shop occupies one corner, an experience bar — a theater of coffee — another. Baristas dress in sleek, ironed aprons sporting a star-above-"R" logo. Customers dish out $8 (or more) for a cup of perfectly brewed coffee. Sitting where your coffee has been roasted, you inhale freshness and sense earthiness. Starbucks markets its Reserve Roasteries as a tribute to the craft of coffee-making: an immersive experience providing temporary escape from the hustle-and-bustle coffee culture, one littered with Unicorn Frappuccinos — and a retreat to a place that respects the sanctity of the simple ($8!) cup of coffee. Yet, despite the homage to coffee, you are simply at the drinking end of long supply chain from earth to cup — a supply chain that includes much more than baristas with tattoos and fedoras.

In most places, coffee is grown on small plots of land and harvested by hand. Coffee pickers may produce 40 pounds of coffee beans per day if they are efficient; the work is difficult, and some may only pick only half that much. They are paid per pound picked. After being picked, coffee beans are dried and hulled and shoveled into jute bags for export. Our cup of coffee is still a long way off.

The first sign that something delicious might be brewing is when coffee is sampled by a human — the "coffee cupper" — who examines it, roasts and grinds a small bit, adds boiling water, "noses" it (to make sure it has the right smell), and finally slurps some before promptly spitting it out to get ready for the next sample. The final steps involve determining which beans to blend and how to roast them — before putting them in roasting machines almost hot enough to melt lead. Finally, the coffee is ground before making its way to shelf or café.

All of which can make us wonder: how is the wealth divided from the United States' $4 billion of coffee imports each year (about 4% of which is fair trade)? Does fair trade really help workers? Some answers to this question are clear, but much remains as cloudy as a coffee with extra cream in it.

Begin with the price of fair trade coffee: are we paying more for it at the counter? We don't know. There is not much data about the prices consumers pay for fair trade coffee compared to conventionally grown coffee comparable in quality, origin, and everything else that might affect a coffee drinker's enjoyment (and its price). Some evidence suggests we're paying more; other evidence suggests we're not. Yet we do know:

1. Fair trade can help small farmers by increasing their income and providing greater economic stability, especially when the market price for coffee has fallen below the price floor.

2. Small, relatively unsophisticated co-operatives are the most likely to become certified fair trade producers. Larger producers may forego fair trade certification for various reasons (such as wanting to use forbidden pesticides).

3. Family incomes rise as fair trade becomes more prevalent. But rising household incomes are only "on average." The economic benefits from fair trade mainly flow to those owning farms or providing skilled work. Unskilled workers (including coffee pickers) do not receive any advantages from fair trade.[43]

The tail wagging the dog

When brewed, a pound of ground coffee might make up to 90 cups. Selling it for just $2 a cup, a coffee shop would receive almost $200. But how much of that do coffee farmers receive? About 200 *times* less. The prices farmers receive are based on what is called the Coffee C-Price — an element of a contract that specifies the price a shipping container of coffee will be bought and sold for at a specific date in the future. This price moves in response to information about the weather, transportation costs, and other factors. The C-Price becomes the benchmark price for all coffee, no matter where it is grown and what its quality, although these considerations are later factored into a particular coffee's actual price.

The C-Price is supposed to make coffee prices less volatile, yet they are far more volatile than the stock market.[44] This wreaks havoc on coffee farmers, who are unable to plan effectively: they might know today's C-Price (and many do), but how does that help them know what it will be after the year it takes to grow and harvest a new crop of coffee, or the four years it takes when you plant new trees? In the face of this uncertainty, farmers act with caution. They are likely to cut back on labor and use more environmentally harmful chemicals. They may attempt to fool certification bodies — whether fair trade, organic, or something else — jeopardizing their certification status. They are often unwilling to risk the outlay of money to invest in technology, even if it might make them more productive.

The C-Price is not set to ensure livable wages for farmers. It is so low that some coffee farmers are giving up their land and migrating with their families to find work. But, while the C-Price pricing mechanism is bad for farmers, it is just fine for the sophisticated commodity traders who trade these coffee contracts on a second-by-second basis. Here, volatility can reward the shrewd coffee speculator. The C-Price also provides a "hedging" strategy for large coffee buyers to protect themselves from swings in coffee prices. Like too many other arrangements linking workers overseas with international markets, the C-Price works well on the corporate side, but creates a high-risk, little-reward proposition for small farmers. They bear the risk of not knowing what prices will be when they harvest. When Starbucks opens profitable new stores, or creates "Reserve" coffees to sell in special cafés for $8 a cup, these windfalls are not "reserved" for farmers.

Even fairer

Concerned organizations are thinking about how to make coffee farming more just and economically sustainable: to make it part of an ecosystem where rewards and risks are more equitably shared. One of these organizations, the non-profit Solidaridad International, writes, "We need to pilot alternative solutions to channel investments to producing countries — solutions that are different than traditional sustainability projects and premiums."[45] Equal Exchange, a partner of Ten Thousand Villages, was one of the first American companies to embrace fair trade coffee. Much as Ten Thousand Villages does, Equal Exchange strives to build relationships with farmers that result in economically just trade benefitting those who grow and harvest coffee. Within its own organization, Equal Exchange's highest-paid employee receives only four times as much as its lowest — more than

90 times less than the typical difference between the earnings of CEOs and their average workers.

But incomes are nowhere close to being equalized across fair trade partners. Fair Trade USA, a standards body, stipulates a principle that would not seem to need mentioning: "Wages and benefits meet or exceed legal minimums." It acknowledges shortcomings even among businesses that may have earned Fair Trade USA certification: "Employers understand [the idea of a] living wage and are implementing a plan to *move towards it* [emphasis mine]." When standards like these are not yet the norm, the development of these aspirations — indeed, expectations — should be commended. Otherwise, they might never be achieved. Fair trade is not just today's cup of coffee. It is a movement.[46]

In the face of all this, should you buy fair trade coffee?

Buying fair trade is not a panacea. Fair trade potentially pays just enough that farmers or growers won't abandon coffee farming for better opportunities, but not enough to escape poverty. Organizations like GiveDirectly (which provide unconditional cash payments to people living in poverty) provide better, more direct support for those living on the far side of our economic fences. But the idea that I might make a difference, even a small one, appeals to me. I think it's more likely I'm doing good than not if I buy fair trade. I think fair trade may be a necessary step to improve an industry that will not be going away.

I buy fair trade.

When I know I'm buying from companies like Ten Thousand Villages or Equal Exchange that are attentive to their suppliers, I try to buy more.

Takeaways from this chapter

Overseas agricultural workers receive some protections from fair trade, though they continue to live hard lives. The price premiums we pay don't guarantee a livable standard of living. But fair trade purchasing still makes sense.

6

TWO-
POCKET
PHILANTHROPY

There are analytical ways to look at doing good and ways that are more intuitive. Both are useful.

Weighing alternatives

We weigh economic alternatives all the time. For two dollars, I can buy a brownie or some carrots. For $15,000, this car or that one. For any given amount of money, I can choose (a) or (b).

For about $200, you could fund five people to receive life-changing (and often -saving) cataract surgeries at India's Aravind Eye Hospital.[47] Or you could treat five girls to a haircut at the beauty shop. Most of us would think using the money at Aravind would do more good.

"Effective altruism" is a development of this logic, with the aim that we "do the *most* good" with our charitable giving. It lets us be dispassionate about choosing a charity. A founder of the effective altruism movement, Peter Singer, poses a question: you have $100,000 to place as a donation: do you use it to improve a local art museum, or do you use it to prevent trachoma, an eye disease in children that leads to blindness by the age of 35.[48] For that amount of money, you could prevent 1,000 children from contracting trachoma or you could create a nicer experience for 100,000 museum-goers (100 times as many beneficiaries). Which donation should you make?

Most of us would give to prevent trachoma, thinking it would do far more good. Here's why, from an effective altruistic perspective. For a moment, suppose you believe this equation is true:

[benefit-per-museum-goer] × [100 museum-goers]
= [benefit-of-sight for 1 person]

(That is, that the benefit [or "good"] from the saving the sight of one person is equal to the combined benefit [good] of 100 people enjoying improvements to the museum.)

So, if you believe the equation, you should be willing to attend the museum yourself if there's a 1-in-100 (1%) chance you would go blind.[49] Most of us would say no to attending the museum under those circumstances, and would still say no if the risk of blindness were 1 in 200, or 500, or 1,000. But maybe you'd feel you would attend if the risk of blindness were 1-in-a-*million* ($\frac{1}{10,000}$%). Which is equivalent to saying that the benefit ("goodness") of sight is one million times greater than the benefit one person receives from attending the nicer museum.

And so, the notional dilemma that Singer proposes is no longer an apples-to-oranges comparison. The numbers tell you to make a donation to trachoma: even though one thousand times fewer people would benefit, that's far, far less than the million-to-one ratio necessary for you to think about contributing to the museum.

This is the essence of effective altruism: determining how much more "good" one outcome is than another; and combining that with how many people receive those benefits to determine the "overall" good from each. And then simply choosing the one that is "best."

When we are faced with a choice like the trachoma–museum example, it would involve some kind of calculation in our minds. Even if we don't do any math to compare impact, some kind of rationalization is being undertaken all the same: I could channel this money (we reason) into either charity X or charity Y, and I have decided on Y, because the money will "do more good." This is effective altruism.

Decisions based on effective altruism often lead to donations to the developing world. One reason for this is that it costs less there to make a difference. A hard-and-fast rule in economics is that dollars lose their value the more of them you get. (Think about someone with a fat bank account and compare them to a child starting a piggy bank.) So money directed overseas can do a lot of good simply because there's less of it there. In addition, some life-enhancing goods and services are quite inexpensive, including drugs that treat or prevent tropical diseases like malaria. Medication that can save a life for a few dollars is an almost unbeatable purchase. (We could actually eliminate malaria, if there were the will to do so, yet it still causes more than 400 thousand deaths each year, many of them in children.)

However, in practice, charitable giving is not governed by effective altruism. In the United States, over $449 billion dollars was given to charity in 2019.[50] Of that amount, religious organizations received almost 30%; the arts, culture, and humanities received 5%; and international affairs and environmental causes received 3% each. Covered under these last two categories are the needs of people in extreme poverty and protecting the planet from catastrophe; effective altruism thinking would have allowed them a much higher percentage.

In short, we don't normally behave like effective altruists. Furthermore, even when we *are* trying to do the most good, we can actually be quite ineffective in the way we give. For example, approaches for addressing and treating HIV/AIDS can vary by a factor of 25 times or more in terms of lives saved per dollar. But, as donors, we may not be able to tell the difference.[51] So, even if we believe we've chosen an important problem to address, it doesn't mean we're backing a good solution.

Today, we can easily find causes to donate to anywhere in the world. But it's not easy to gauge their effectiveness. This creates space for GiveWell.org (and similar organizations), which look for the most effective charities with the same passion with which stock pickers identify undervalued stocks or foodies discover new restaurants. Itself a nonprofit, GiveWell collects and evaluates evidence about other charities. How much better do they make people's lives, or the planet? Are their solutions efficient? Can they put additional money to good use? Few of us can answer those questions ourselves, so GiveWell can help us do more good with our giving. To be clear: this approach is different from rating charities by their "administrative efficiency," where high ratings are awarded where a large percentage of their donations goes toward direct support of their cause (rather than on internal expenses). This latter approach is used by other charity evaluation websites, however.

Organizations that can help us make charitable decisions are listed in Appendix 4.

Heart and the unknown

There are good reasons not to follow the cold, hard logic of effective altruism. For a start, it could lead to conclusions you don't agree with. In a burning house, should you save a child or a Picasso? A die-hard effective altruism argument might favor the Picasso, so that you could then sell it and use the money to save the lives of more than one child. This probably isn't compatible with your sense of right and wrong (nor mine). This is the kind of problem that moral philosophers have struggled with for a long time.

Or let's think again about trachoma and the art museum. What if the museum were, instead, the National Museum of African American History and Culture? Or the United States Holocaust Memorial Museum? Both help people connect with their heritage; both serve as vivid reminders of how fragile our human rights are. How "beneficial" are those things? Who gets to decide? How much does our own race or religion matter in answering these questions? Visiting these museums — or any museums — can open our hearts; open hearts bring us together. The ripples expanding from this we can only imagine.

Even if you take an effective altruism perspective, you might still be willing to give a lot of money for a cause you're familiar with but only a tiny amount for something you've never heard of. Maybe it's misleading even to pose a question like "Should you give $100,000 to a museum or to combat trachoma?" because in real life no one will ever face a decision like that.

There are situations in which I will try to act like an effective altruist, but many in which I won't. Once you realize how often you might potentially need to be that effective altruist, you recognize how overwhelming it could become. Do I need a cost–benefit analysis to justify giving a bit of money to a Salvation Army Santa or to a local, non-profit summer camp? Or is that a requirement only when I'm justifying giving considerably more money to combat a dreaded disease like dengue fever? And, no matter the math, I like giving to enable kids to go to that camp. When I support the summer camp, I'm supporting my neighborhood. It makes me think a little more fondly of where I live. It gives pleasure to the campers, and to their parents, my neighbors. And what if my own kids go there? In that case, my charitable donation is contributing to my own children's enjoyment. So now is it really charity anymore? It gets confusing.

What about contributions to churches or related institutions (temples, mosques, a meditation center)? Members may receive deep, spiritual connections or guidance from these institutions; these donations can be heartfelt and meaningful. (And recall that this is where nearly one-third of charitable dollars end up.) Yet some contributions may go toward air-conditioned buses or a fresh coat of paint. What feels sacred to you may not appear so to me. Each of us can draw our own line around what is acceptable.

Both–and

One way to help us get a handle on our charitable decisions is the two-pocket approach: we imagine putting the dollars we want to give into different pockets. In one pocket I can put money for things that make me feel good: supporting that summer camp; supporting a girl scout next door (or is it just about the cookies?); giving to the art museum, where I sometimes go over lunch; or to a concert house where I listen to music; or a street newspaper because I know the founder; or to any number of non-profits I appreciate. My other pocket is the "pure charity" pocket. With the money I put there I can try to do as much good as possible. With these dollars, I can embrace effective altruism.

What should we take from all this? How do we "do good" philanthropically? Some thoughts:

1. Keep straight the money you put in your two charitable pockets. Having money in both is fine, but think about how you allocate money between them.

2. Don't make judgments about charities based solely on their overhead: the amount they spend on salaries, advertising, and everything else not directly related to the support they provide. It is possible that highly paid staff and expensive, but effective, advertising can do much more good than they cost.[52]

3. Don't be taken in by emotions (alone). If an advertisement puts a lump in your throat, you're probably not the only one. That means that, even if you don't give to that cause, many others still might because they got lumps in their throats as well. (But let your heart speak to you, too.)

4. Your money can do the most *measurable* good when given to organizations that (a) effectively (b) address important problems (c) that are underfunded, and (d) can put the donations they receive to effective use. (These are the hallmarks of effective altruism.)

5. Effective altruism can be used to evaluate U.S. charities, if that is where you want to give.

6. Some effective altruists suggest an "earn to give" strategy: take a job — even something you find lacking in social value, possibly soul-crushing — because you'll earn a lot and can put more money in your "pure charity" pocket. I don't think that I would recommend this to my loved ones, but it might resonate with you. Think about this strategy with care before you adopt it.

Giving charitably means acting with generosity. We may use our heads, but generosity comes from our hearts. We can find opportunities for generosity in other aspects of our lives, too — with our time, our listening, our empathy, or our support, just for starters. Acting with generosity brings us closer; it links us together — this, on top of all the outward good it can do.[53]

Takeaways from this chapter

The principles of *effective altruism* can guide us in contributing to charities that put our money to extremely good (measurable) use. Charitable donations that don't meet the test of effective altruism may nonetheless create impact in important ways that are harder to measure.

DON'T BANK ON IT

Few of us pay much attention to where we bank. But some banks take your money and put it to work for causes you care about, while others use your money in ways you'd almost certainly disapprove of.

This chapter begins with a brief look at what banking used to be like until large, mega-banks transformed the industry. I present this so we can understand how impersonal banking has become and see what the effects have been. The latter part of this chapter explains how we can still find banks that serve societal interests, as banks used to do, even if there are fewer of them. We have choices about where we bank, and these choices make a difference. A list of tools to help you find banks (and their near relatives) that "do good" is found in Appendix 5.

Big banks overtake small banks

Savings and Loans (S&Ls) were once the mainstay of home-ownership, funding almost all home mortgage loans 50 years ago. (If you know the movie, think of *It's a Wonderful Life*, starring Jimmy Stewart and Donna Reed.) S&Ls raised the money to fund home loans by offering attractive interest rates to savers in their communities in federally insured savings accounts. They served as the nation's banks.

Then, all that changed. Legislation was passed which, for the first time, allowed banks to acquire banks in other states. A system of nationwide banks arose. These new banks were also entitled to offer higher interest rates to savers than S&Ls could. S&L customers fled to these new banks, or put their money in high-interest money-market accounts. In two years, S&Ls went from being profitable to losing $4 billion a year. Then a series of risky investments caused thousands of S&Ls to close. In just over 15 years, the number of S&Ls dropped from more than 3,200 to fewer than 1,000.

All of this resulted in drastic shifts in where our deposits are held. In 1995, small and medium banks (and credit unions) held 60% of all deposits. They now hold less than 25%.[54] Now, four enormous *mega*-banks alone hold over 50% of the nation's deposits. Even during the decade *after* the financial crisis of 2007–2009 (in which large banks played a starring role), the three largest banks *added* $2.4 trillion in holdings, an increase of 180%.[55]

The drop in locally held deposits hollowed out communities. The new banks are not designed to support them.

Wall Street overtakes Main Street

In addition to commercial banks, where everyday people bank, there are investment banks that cater to the needs of wealthy business clients. These banks raise money to fund all kinds of investments, everywhere in the world.

In 1999, federal legislation permitted banks to stir together their investment banking activities and their everyday, commercial banking. (This had been prohibited since the Great Depression to protect everyday bankers from risk.) Investment banks could now take people's savings and put them to use as investments in huge corporations. Large commercial banks became "universal banks" — meaning that they, too, could act like investment banks.

Relentless lobbying resulted in banking becoming riskier and more speculative. Lenders began providing housing loans that people could never afford; the investment banks cut those loans into tiny pieces, scrambling them into a financial hash they hoped would hide its rotting ingredients. The result was the financial crisis and Great Recession beginning December 2007. Nearly ten million families lost their homes. Unemployment doubled from 5% to 10%. All told, Americans lost an estimated $9.8 trillion in wealth as the value of their houses and retirement accounts collapsed.[56] Yet the financial crisis consolidated the banking industry more than ever, further diverting attention away from the everyday financial needs of Main Street.

Here's what is important to understand: if you have money in a bank, the bank is going to use it — somehow. Large, name-brand banks are the least likely to use your money in ways that are attentive to the environment, civil rights, or other social issues of concern to many people today. Smaller, local banks will.

Large banks' investments deepen the climate crisis, a topic discussed in the next chapter ("Cut Them Up"), which focuses on credit cards and their relationship to banking. (In that chapter you will find suggestions for finding new credit card options.)

The current chapter focuses on how small banks are especially effective at supporting local communities. In the next three sections, we'll look at the importance of small banks in making small business loans, home loans (mortgages), and in letting money re-circulate within a community. The remainder of the chapter will talk about the choices we have about moving our money to local financial institutions.

Small business loans

Due to their scale and geographic reach, and enabled by technology, large banks now use an algorithmic approach to review loan applications. This means a loan application will be processed almost instantly and with very little labor — which banks like. But these decisions are made without any actual knowledge of the applicants, or a community's needs and histories. This formulaic approach results in fewer small business loans, since many loan candidates don't fit algorithms' exact criteria and will be denied. We are seeing the number of loans banks make for $1 million or more soaring (they fit the algorithms' criteria), loans to small businesses falling, and loans to "micro" business vanishing.[57]

Unlike large banks, small banks know their customers personally. To a small bank a loan applicant might appear as what she is: a hardworking, committed business owner. Small banks sense, and want to support, a community's business and financial needs. They lend to the kinds of applicants big banks turn away.

For almost every year in the last two decades, small banks have made better loan decisions than giant banks. Small banks and credit unions were making *two to three times* fewer bad loans (defaults on payments), on a percentage basis, than large banks around the time of the financial crisis. Their default rate for home mortgages was 16 times less than the average for all banks.[58] Small banks are performing better than banks 100 times their size.[59]

Small banks shoulder an unusually high percentage of small business loans. They can often put 20 times more of their money (as a percentage) to work supporting small businesses than giant banks do. Community-based financial institutions control just 16% of the industry's assets, but they are responsible for 52% of small business lending.[60]

Despite small banks' efforts, small businesses are unable to borrow enough money. Fewer than half of the small businesses seeking loans get the money they need. When denied, they may resort to high-cost alternatives (short-term loans with very high interest rates; or sometimes loan sharks or payday lenders). Many small businesses simply go out of business. Minority business owners are at a special disadvantage, with close to one in ten needing to dig into their personal funds when they can't get a loan, despite being less wealthy than average to begin with.[61] On average, banks discourage nearly 50% of Black business owners from even applying for a loan (compared to about 15% of White business owners), and only 40% get the amount they request (versus over 65% for White business owners).

Putting our money on deposit with local financial institutions can support the provision of more, and more inclusive, small business loans.

Home mortgages

Homeownership is a foundation for building personal wealth. Homeownership can increase personal wealth by $10,000 or more per year, though the average is lower for people who are Black or Hispanic.[62] To buy a home, you take out a loan called a home mortgage.

For most people lucky enough to own a home, it is their most valuable asset. As a rule, lower-income individuals either have wealth from owning a home or they have no wealth at all.[63] Sadly, more and more of the population is finding itself in the "no wealth at all" category. Shifts in the banking industry have put homeownership out of reach for too many. Among those without a college education, home-ownership has dropped 10% in a few decades.[64] And people who are Black or of Color have suffered the most. During the housing scandal preceding the financial crisis, they were often the targets of subprime mortgages — which were very risky and often resulted in people losing their homes.[65]

What can we do?

When we bank at local banks, we provide them with money that they use to create mortgages. As we've noted, these banks see creditworthiness where larger banks' algorithms don't. And they make better loan decisions. So, when we bank at small local banks, we make homeownership possible for more people.

Leakage

Once money leaves your community, it loses its power as an economic multiplier. (Remember from Chapter 4, "Stay

Home," how money spent locally re-circulates, every dollar contributing an extra 50 cents.) The corollary of that is money that "leaks" from a community, which does not provide that extra — important — kick. Dollars either re-circulate or leak out of a community, depending on where you bank.

When banks make loans to the communities in which they operate, funds are re-circulating: a depositor's money may fund the expansion of a local hardware store or provide a mortgage for a nearby home. Money is much less likely to re-circulate when banks are regional or national. Make a deposit with Citibank in Buffalo, NY, and decisions about how your money is used will be made in New York City, where Citibank has its headquarters. Make a deposit at Fifth Third Bank in New Buffalo, MI, and decisions will be made in Cincinnati. When decision-makers are based outside your hometown, don't expect them to prioritize your community's needs; their decisions will be made on strictly financial criteria.

Leakage analyses look at economic flows out of a community. When a community could have produced some good or service in a cost-effective way — but "imported" it instead — there is avoidable leakage. Economically healthy communities practice "LOIS": locally owned import substitution.[66] When it makes sense to do so, they avoid unnecessary imports. When it comes to banking, too, there are alternatives to large (imported) national and regional banks, which are harmful to local communities.

Few communities conduct a leakage analysis, but those that do realize that leakage from financial systems quickly drains their community's wealth.[67] In East Oakland, CA, persistent poverty was linked to $40–50 million annually flowing to non-local banks as interest payments on mortgages.

The state of Vermont found it was leaking half a billion dollars a year on mortgage interest payments — on top of $1.5 billion leaked by insurance premiums, and a quarter-billion dollars leaked from interest payments to out-of-state banks. Turn this around and we get more self-reliant communities, with stronger small business and mortgage lending.

How we can do this is the next topic.

Financial activism

On April 3, 1968, the night before he was assassinated, Dr. Martin Luther King gave a speech in Memphis, Tennessee. The occasion was to support the city's striking sanitation workers and their call for better pay and safer working conditions after two garbage collectors had been crushed to death by a malfunctioning truck. The speech is remembered for its most famous line, "I've been to the mountaintop." But Dr. King's speech was in fact urging a broad agenda of economic and social justice. Less poetic were his words asking people to spend more intentionally:

> [W]e are asking you tonight to go out and tell your neighbors not to buy Coca-Cola in Memphis. . . . [T]ell them not to buy Sealtest milk. Tell them not to buy . . . Wonder Bread.[68]

These companies were singled out because of their unfair hiring practices. Dr. King then trained his focus on financial institutions:

> But not only that, we've got to strengthen Black institutions. I call upon you to take your money out of the banks downtown and deposit your money

in Tri-State Bank. We want a "bank-in" movement in Memphis. Go by the savings and loan association. I'm not asking you something that we don't do ourselves at SCLC [the Southern Christian Leadership Conference, his organization]. ... [W]e have an account here in the savings and loan association from the Southern Christian Leadership Conference. We are telling you to follow what we are doing. Put your money there. You have six or seven Black insurance companies here in the city of Memphis. Take out your insurance there. We want to have an "insurance-in."[69]

Dr. King understood the power of economic mobilization. Today, too, our financial actions send a message — and make a difference.

We have choices about where to bank, choices with implications, yet this is something most of us never appreciate. Opening a new bank account is something you can do from your kitchen table. Many banks let you open an account online or with a phone call, in less time than you can drink a cup of coffee. And these banks don't have to be in your backyard, or even the state where you live. You can choose a bank that supports a cause you care about — community development, poverty alleviation, a greener planet, Black Lives Matter, to name a few. If you wanted, you could open a new account with three, four, or five banks — each with a different emphasis (it's perfectly legal) — depositing some of your money in each.

MLK was deliberate in choosing where his organization would bank. The rest of this chapter describes some of the choices we have for our personal banking.

Local banks

Banking at a locally owned and run bank is an easy way to support your community. Local *ownership* of a bank means it is far more likely that dollars you deposit will be reinvested in the community. Locally *run* means that credit decisions very likely take into account local knowledge, not just FICO scores and other formal calculations of creditworthiness. And, thus, these banks will give loans to small businesses (and people) that might otherwise be denied credit by large banks.

Local banks offer consumers the same conveniences as other banks, including mobile and online banking. Their fees may be *lower*, but they will not have physical branches outside your community; and their ATM networks may be smaller. Unless you are a business customer seeking a customized loan, the products and services offered by a local bank are the same as from any other bank.

Although the number of community banks is in decline, it remains fairly easy to find a bank that serves local needs. Using online tools, you can examine a bank on factors like: location of the bank's headquarters, its size and ownership structure, the percentage of its assets devoted to small business and small farm lending, the percentage of its business that is focused on local markets, and its use of deposits for speculative investment rather than local reinvestment. You can also learn banks' overall impact scores.

Appendix 5 has a list of tools to help you find an appropriate local bank or other financial institution.

Credit unions

Credit unions are non-profit, member-owned (co-operative) financial institutions. Most are local. In 2018, there were 5,530 federally insured credit unions in the United States, with combined assets of over $1.4 trillion.[70] That's about as much as one of the country's mega-banks. Consolidation is reducing the number of credit unions, but their combined assets continue to increase. Most credit unions offer customers the same products, services, and amenities as banks.

Several factors distinguish credit unions from banks. Because they are non-profit, they are not trying to make as much money as possible; and they pay no taxes. As a result, the fees they charge you are typically lower. So are their mortgage rates. They pay you more interest on your savings account. And the profits they make are returned to members in the form of dividends, rather than being paid to stockholders. Credit unions are owned by their members, and members (whom banks would call customers) get an unusual say in running the business. Every member gets exactly one vote in selecting the credit union's board of directors, no matter how much money he or she has on deposit or the number of loans they've already taken. (The board is a group of volunteers who are in charge of the credit union's direction and assume responsibilities for its activities.) Members also vote on other issues needing approval.

Community development credit unions (also called low-income credit unions) have a stated mission to provide financial services to low- and moderate-income people and their communities. They offer loans at fair prices, even to people without sterling credit ratings, and sometimes to those with no credit history at all. Their aim is to provide a means for individuals to escape cycles of debt and begin to save money. (Community development credit unions also belong to a family of financial institutions known as CDFIs, a topic we will visit shortly.)

In every local credit union, a member's deposits help others in the community to whom the credit union makes loans. Credit unions, like other community-based financial institutions, shoulder a disproportionately large share of local, small-business lending. They may offer a variety business loans.

B Corp banks

A handful of banks have earned B Corp certification. Like any other for-profit, a bank's B Corp eligibility is determined by evaluating its impact on its workers, community, and the environment, as well as its internal governance. Banks that have received B Corp certification differ markedly from one another, but all are determined to use finance to serve societal ends. What follows are descriptions of two B Corp banks. I offer a fairly deep dive into the first, Beneficial State Bank, to capture the breadth of what B Corp banking can mean. I give a briefer description of the other, Aspiration, to show how even startup banks are striving to turn banking upside down.

Beneficial State Bank is tugging the banking industry with all its might toward a fairer, more equitable future. Headquartered in Oakland, it believes that a new kind of banking is essential for a healthy economy and just world — and it is determined to show everyone the way. It believes banking must be fully inclusive, racially and gender just, and environmentally regenerative — ideas it has put into action to achieve B Corp certification. Founded in 2007, Beneficial State Bank operates under the philosophy that a bank that serves societal goals can not only survive but thrive. By acting in this way, Beneficial State hopes to serve as a model for other banks to follow.

Beneficial State Bank is owned by a non-profit foundation. As a result, it will never have private shareholders whose motives are to maximize the bank's profit. All dividends the foundation receives from Beneficial State's profits are reinvested in low-income communities or to support environmental causes. While gigantic banks hold more than one thousand times the assets apiece than it does, Beneficial State believes it is creating a model that larger regional banks will find irresistible. Its plan is to win "market share wars" by making only investments that align with the social justice values important to an increasing number of citizens, including stronger inner cities, improving health and wellness for everyone, and protecting the environment. Beneficial State sees itself as David in a struggle with Goliath, but writing a playbook others will follow.

Beneficial State is also a CDFI bank (a topic discussed below), which means that 60% of its loans must be made to low-income census tracts. But its own standards state that it must give 75% or more of its loans to "changemaker" organizations, including companies engaged in renewable energy, and to co-operatively owned businesses. It will never make loans contrary to its own values, such as for for-profit prisons or fossil fuels. It also pledges to pay its workers at least 150% of the regionally adjusted livable wage, obtain third-party validation for its social impact, reduce its carbon footprint, and fully disclose its efforts to influence legislation.

Despite being non-profit-owned, Beneficial State is a for-profit bank. It aims to consistently make a return on its equity of at least 6% (to make sure it is financially sustainable), but never more than 10% (because too great a profit would mean it is either overcharging its customers or underpaying its employees). Its triple-bottom-line approach is in stark contrast to large, commercial banks whose profit-hungry practices are at the expense of the economy at large, communities everywhere, and the health of the planet. Beneficial State's ambition is nothing short of changing the entire banking system — the system that makes the economy go.

Aspiration, another — very different — type of B Corp bank, opened its doors in 2015, advertising, "Save Money, Save the Planet." It now has over five million customers. It complements this slogan with no ATM fees anywhere and a "Pay What is Fair" model under which its clients determine what their fees will be for banking services. Aspiration is a completely online "bank" (it's not actually a bank, but you'd never know it), founded in partnership with a community bank in Boston. It donates 10% of its revenue to U.S. microfinance institutions, it routes customer deposits to local banks throughout the U.S. that are certified as fossil-free, and generally supports its clients' desires to use their money to focus on the environment, society, and good corporate behavior.[71]

Appealing to the tech-savvy, the bank's Aspiration Impact Measurement (AIM) tool gives its customers feedback on all their purchases. By examining 75,000 data points, it lets them know how any of the 5,000 tracked companies they might have purchased from scores on its behavior toward its employees, the communities in which it operates, and environment. AIM lets *us* know how we stack up as socially responsible *consumers*, too.[72]

Community Development Financial Institutions (CDFIs)

Community development financial institutions (CDFIs) can be: local banks, credit unions, loan funds, or venture capital funds supporting small to medium businesses in low-income communities. In order to be designated as a CDFI, an organization must assure the U.S. Treasury that it supports the financial needs of a community overlooked or underserved by ordinary financial institutions. The Treasury also provides CDFIs with some of their funding.

CDFIs are part of a tradition stretching back more than a hundred years in the United States. When banks in Manhattan's Lower East Side refused to provide credit to immigrants in the late 1800s, immigrant guilds stepped into the breach.[73] In the early days of the Great Depression, African American communities formed the first community development credit unions. These efforts resemble the "self-help" efforts that have arisen in all parts of the world, for centuries, where peers (often women) offer each other financial support.

CDFIs began to take their current form in the 1960s and '70s, supporting efforts such as the "War on Poverty." In 1994, a fund was established by the federal government to provide competitive funding for CDFIs. Notably, the Community Reinvestment Act was revised in 1995, a revision that allows banks to satisfy their Community Reinvestment obligations (which gives them banking privileges) by making loans or other investments in CDFIs.[74] This greatly expanded their numbers.

Today there are approximately 1,200 CDFIs, operating in all 50 states. About a half of them are loan funds.[75] Together they have approximately $100 billion in assets, which they use to meet the unserved financial needs of low-income communities by making small business and home loans, and helping create jobs with decent wages. Some CDFIs offer programs on managing money or starting a business.

Just as with other banks or credit unions, it is possible to open an account at a CDFI bank (or "community development bank") or at a CDFI credit union. You will enjoy the same services you are accustomed to: checking accounts (often with interest higher than at banks), certificates of deposit, debit and credit cards, and online banking.[76]

Almost banking

You can provide money to a CDFI bank or credit union by interacting with a third party, and be repaid with interest — in effect, making the CDFI a loan. As one example, Calvert Impact Capital, Inc., a non-profit, makes its Community Investment Notes available for the public to purchase.[77] Essentially, your money flows through Calvert to one of its "impact partners": organizations and funds that work in financially underserved areas to provide better financial services related to issues like affordable housing, women's empowerment, improved education, and climate justice. You can designate specific sectors you choose to support with the note.[78] The note you purchase can be as small as $20, for a term of between six months and 20 years. You get a competitive interest rate, but these notes carry the slight risk of not being fully repaid.

Bank on this

Our financial system moves vast sums around the globe in the blink of an eye's blink of an eye by routing money through banks and other financial institutions. This financial wiring contributes to many of the problems we see around us: staggering concentrations of wealth co-existing with entrenched poverty; financing available for fossil fuel but not small business; being less likely to get a loan today because of who your ancestors were 400 years ago.

That is the old system — the existing system. But a newer and better system can emerge — is emerging — when we put our mind, and money, into it.

Takeaways from this chapter

Most banks invest your money in things you may not like. Local banks, credit unions, and CDFIs are much less likely to do so; plus they invest in local economies — unlike large national banks, which will whisk your money away once they get it. Banks are not all the same, and you can choose to bank anywhere . Some banks are B Corp certified, which means a commitment to workers, community, and the environment.

8 CUT THEM UP

The idea behind a purchase is simple: I get something I want from you (say, a book), and you take my money. That's the end of it. Both of us feel we've come away better off. I might anticipate reasons I'll regret the purchase later — the book might become just another doorstop. But what you do with the money is none of my concern. Yet this representation is incomplete. All money lives a life beyond our purchases. This chapter takes a look at how.

But, first, here's another example: I'm planning a trip abroad and I book a flight. I provide my credit card information and check this off my To-Do list. Finis.

However, a lot more is going on here. I'm adding to Delta's revenue. Delta kicks a few bucks back to my credit card company for processing the transaction. I get to use its card because I pay a few hundred dollars a year for it (and I get great miles). And, every so often, I'm nicked with fees and interest payments on top of my annual fee. So what about that credit card company? What does it do with the money? To explore that question, it's useful to look at the cattle ranching and soy industries, the two major culprits in the destruction of the Amazon rainforest. And then at the fossil fuel industry and its quest for profit over planet. Then we'll return to credit cards.

The out-of-control fires in the Amazon may seem like prehistory (they were daily front-page headlines during summer–fall of 2019) given more recent threats: a pandemic, recession, racial unrest, and too many people, including people in power, intent on snuffing out democracy, or looking the other way. But the fires are not yesterday's news. They still burn and represent (and accelerate) the destruction of the world's largest rainforest. Some describe the Amazon as "the world's lungs." They breathe in carbon dioxide, they breathe out oxygen — we get 20% of our oxygen in this way.

A felled tree loses the ability to take CO_2 out of the air. Plus, it will release all the carbon it has been capturing if it is burned or left to rot. Deforestation has reduced tree cover in the Amazon by about 20% over the last half-century — something close to removing half a lung.[79] In one year, beginning August 2019, an area more than three-fourths the size of Connecticut was destroyed.[80] The international banking and financial system funds this activity, and more.

Cattle ranching in Brazil, home to more than half of the rainforest, accounts for about 80% of the Amazon's deforestation, most of it illegal. Ranchers raise the cattle, meat processors do the dirty work of slaughtering animals for meat and leather, and still other companies sell these products in markets overseas.

Consider JBS, the Brazilian meat-processing company. JBS's U.S. operations gained notoriety for demanding that its employees continue to work while the Covid epidemic was ripping through U.S. slaughterhouses, infecting more than 3,000 workers; the company hoped to avoid reducing the number of cattle it could "process" per day (currently 80,000, worldwide). The investment bank JPMorgan has assisted JBS as it has acquired other giant meat-packing companies to become the largest meat processor in the world. JPMorgan has also helped JBS sell bonds to raise money to further expand its reach.[81] Enormous financial firms including Fidelity and BlackRock have invested billions of dollars in JBS stock.

Growing soy also contributes to the deforestation of the Amazon, as well as the neighboring Cerrado biome — which has suffered 50% more deforestation than the Amazon for over a decade.[82] Soy is Brazil's largest agricultural export, and Brazilian soy, like the country's meat and leather, finds its way to foreign markets: China, Europe, and the United States. Large, international corporations are involved in these transactions, just as they are in the beef industry. Cargill and ADM — huge U.S. companies — deliver Brazilian soy around the world. To finance these efforts, JPMorgan and Bank of America have each provided both firms over $1 billion apiece in credit and other financial support in a five-year period.

While the Amazon supports life by removing the carbon dioxide the world desperately needs out of the atmosphere, we continue to bellow it out with powerful indifference. The world has fallen short of every target science has set to try to prevent climate disaster. A 2°C rise in the Earth's average temperature was once considered disastrous. It is now an ambition that is essentially out of reach.[83]

Fossil fuels and the industry they power are the largest contributors to carbon dioxide in the atmosphere. As early as the mid-1970s, Exxon conducted internal research that established the link between burning fossil fuels and rising temperatures on Earth — then tried to convince the public until very recently that there was no basis for concern.[84] No one grieves for the days of whale oil. But the fossil fuel industry today just won't let us quit our hydrocarbons. Unimaginably powerful lobbyists have politicians in their hip pockets to protect oil and gas companies' interests.[85] Getting fossil fuel companies to cease or even curtail their activities would negatively impact their revenue, so they'll fight to extract every ounce of profit from every drop of gas and oil they can produce. Yet, as environmentalists like Bill McKibben and environmental protection agencies like Amazon Watch have pointed out, we can exert powerful leverage in combating the climate crisis by pressuring financial institutions to stop their harmful investments. The organization that McKibben founded, 350.org, provides inspiration for climate activists and lists ongoing efforts we can join. (The "350" is a reference to the maximum safe concentration [in parts per million] of carbon in the atmosphere. We are currently above 400, the highest level in about three million years.)

JPMorgan is the world's largest funder of fossil fuels. It announced with much self-congratulation that it would stop funding new oil and gas exploration projects in the Arctic — yet it continues to fund the companies that undertake them, still supports exploration and development in other parts of the world, and remains invested in "emerging" (and decidedly non-green) technologies including fracking, tar sands, and oil and gas pipelines.[86] JPMorgan has plenty of company: the 60 largest banks poured $3.8 trillion (yes, *trillion*) into fossil fuel financing via direct loans and other means between 2016 and 2020.[87] Despite Covid driving down demand for fossil fuel in 2020, it was still higher than in 2016.

The names of the culprits in the climate crisis may be both familiar and new: oil and gas companies, of course — Shell, ExxonMobil, and Sinopec (a Chinese firm, with the largest revenues) — along with dark-money lobbying groups, whose pleasant-sounding, Orwellian names like American Prosperity Institute and Honest Elections Project shield identities (such as the Koch Brothers and the DeVos family, respectively) from public view. Add to this list the top fossil-fuel bankers: JPMorgan, Citi, Wells Fargo, and Bank of America, ranking #1, #2, #3, and #4.[88]

If JPMorgan ceased all its fossil fuel investments, it would need to adjust only 7% of its investment portfolio. But, with only that small adjustment, Exxon could be blocked from taking us further down a path of climate ruin. (We would see a similar pattern if JPMorgan withheld funds from Cargill, ADM, JBS, and others in the soy and cattle industries who are destroying the Amazon and other regions vital for life on Earth.[89] In short, huge banks hold the cards when it comes to financing the industrial-scale destruction of the planet. And they are using our money.[90]

My flight arranged, I receive my credit card statement. It shows the $843 I was charged for my flight from Detroit to London. Delta will give me "miles" for the flight (bonus). And Chase gives me 3× points for using its Chase Sapphire Reserve card — the "best travel card in the industry" according to reviews (huge bonus).

Chase? . . . As in JPMorgan Chase? As in banker of Amazon deforestation? As in banker to the fossil fuel industry? Yes . . . as in JPMorgan Chase.

Recall that this chapter began by mentioning that Delta will share some of the money I spent with my credit card company, Chase, in the form of an "interchange fee," a fee of about 1–3%. The more lavish a card's rewards, the higher the interchange fee.[91] Delta's bank will also take another, smaller piece of this transaction, often a fixed fee of less than $1.

One neglected effect of banks taking their cut is that Delta, like other merchants, will raise its prices to compensate. Credit card holders don't lose out, it would appear, because the slight bit more we're spending gives us points toward our next vacations. But, in a way, when I charge my Delta flight on my Chase card, it makes flying a bit more expensive for everyone, including the 60% of low-income Americans who have credit cards but whose credit ratings don't qualify them for the same rewards.

But back to Chase. You may recall from the last chapter ("Don't Bank on It") that banks are now allowed by law to mix their retail banking and their investment banking. The fees we pay for our credit cards can be used to fund things we are vehemently opposed to, like the destruction of the Amazon and an economy clinging to fossil fuels. JPMorgan Chase uses our money the way it wants to — to make as much money as possible — paying little attention to what its credit card holders might want. And they act no differently than any other major bank that issues its own credit cards.

Though we might not find it a painless thing to do, we can cut those credit cards — cut them to pieces and replace them with cards that still provide us credit but are not connected to the kinds of destructive investments we might be unwittingly supporting. We may not get the same points, but let's forfeit them in exchange for the hope of a habitable planet in generations to come.

However, be alert to the fact that the major card companies might try to fool you into thinking you're doing more good than you really are. Most offer affiliate cards. Bank of America cards might display the WWF logo along with photos of cute polar bears, frolicking pandas, inscrutable leopards, and tigers beseeching us to "do something nice for me." But the amount that WWF receives when the card is used is only a tiny slice compared to the fees that Bank of America itself receives. And Bank of America still gets to use the money in its investment banking division, BoA Securities, whose investments we may abhor. Bank of America is simply acting like other card issuers, who support a wide range of affiliate rewards programs — not only WWF, but also The Nature Conservancy, Susan G. Koman, Major League Baseball, and USAA's Wounded Warrior Project, not to mention everyone's favorite "charity": AOL. And lest we forget, there is the erstwhile Hello Kitty Visa.[92]

If we don't want our credit cards financing projects that lead to ecological destruction or economic or social injustice — if want them to *do good* — then what can we do? Here's where community banks help us again. Recall how differently they act when it comes to supporting local communities compared to their larger, national cousins. Because their loans go to hardware stores, shoe stores, and brew pubs, they don't have the inclination to invest in Amazon deforestation or Shell Oil's next project. Even if they did, their charters would prevent it. Community development banks' credit cards are especially attractive if you'd like to support investments in low-income areas. Appendix 5 lists tools for finding banks and other institutions whose credit cards try to avoid doing damage or strive to do good.

Credit unions offer credit cards, too. But, because every credit union reflects its membership, they may have drastically different personalities. One credit union that receives high scores for its rates, fees, and rewards is Boeing Employees Credit Union. It's not hard to imagine them dreaming about cheap, plentiful fossil fuel. So, choose a credit union card with care.

B Corp Banks also issue credit cards. Remember: these banks have received a passing B Impact Assessment score covering their workers, their community, the environment, and their internal governance. Almost without question, these institutions reflexively oppose activities that aggravate the climate crisis.[93] Aspiration, the completely online B Corp bank, flashes its pro-social bona fides prominently on its "Spend and Save" web page.[94] The first thing you see is "Save Money, Save the Planet." What does that mean to you? And is it worth it if you won't be getting the "points" you've come to expect? Aspiration's debit card offers advantages quite different from those you'd get from a Chase card. You can learn about the environmental and social performance of all the companies you're buying from. You get up to 10% cash back when you buy from select companies striving to "do good" — including Reformation (sustainable fashion), TOMS (footwear), Goodwings (hotel bookings), Arcadia Power (utility bills), Imperfect Foods (avoiding food waste), and others. When you buy gas, the carbon from your driving will be completely offset. Aspiration's "Plant Your Change" option lets customers round up their purchases to the nearest dollar (e.g., $23.47 become $24), with the excess (here, 53¢) going to plant trees. Over three million trees have already been planted, and all tree plantings are all conducted in conjunction with verified carbon reduction projects.

Does this even need mentioning? Funds on deposit with Aspiration will never be used to support the fossil fuel industry.

Or this? The choices we make about credit and debit cards can make a world of difference.

Takeaways from this chapter

Credit cards funnel your money into investments that you may abhor. Cards with the best perks are often issued to favor those with money, penalizing the less affluent. Cards issued by certain banks and other financial institutions use our money in socially and environmentally enlightened ways.

INVESTING FOR REAL IMPACT

Impact investing has become a thing — albeit a thing without a tight definition. Some impact investors are looking for something "good" to invest in but which still generates a handsome profit. Others see impact investing as supporting ventures you can't profit from but investing in them anyway because they are worthy. What all definitions have in common is that they consider societal impact alongside financial return, but they do so to varying degrees.

Impact investing wasn't a name anyone used until the Rockefeller Foundation coined the term a decade into this century, but the idea has been around much longer. A loan is an investment, and CDFIs (for example) have been providing loans to underserved businesses and communities for decades. It just wasn't called impact investing then. Today, we can all put our money to work through CDFIs or take part in impact investing in a variety of other ways if we want to. That's what this chapter is about.

It's easy to stick a toe in. The online lending platform Kiva.org lists underserved businesses around the world that are seeking money to grow or sometimes simply to stay in business. Online lenders — like you or me — fund these loans in $25 increments. The loans may assist an entrepreneur who is just getting her footing, or they may enable a more established business to expand its inventory or invest in better equipment. Loans to businesses are small — averaging about $400 — but over $1.5 billion has been lent in this way. Online lenders are repaid 96% of the time, but without interest. On repayment, many lenders use the money to make another Kiva loan.

If you want to *grow* your money while still considering the societal implications of your investment, you need other options. The most common way for people to invest is by buying stock or a mutual fund (bundle of stocks), and you can do that in ways that do good — or at least refrain from doing bad.

There have been a number of companies mentioned in these pages that try to do good. If they're public companies — meaning they have stock (or "shares") you can buy on a stock exchange — we can invest in them. But is there a systematic way to identify "good" companies to invest in? There are no absolute standards to guide us, and there are different philosophies. One well-known philosophy, *socially responsible investing* (SRI), identifies "sin stocks" and rules them out. Sin is in the eye of the beholder, but many people would say that companies involved in weapons, tobacco, or for-profit prisons are sinful, and so are their stocks. But is alcohol sinful? What about cannabis? It all ultimately comes down to our own personal values. Whatever remains after you've ruled out "sin" comprises the companies you can invest in, according to the SRI philosophy; of course, you should always consider a company's financial side if you're trying to make money. Appendix 6 provides links to all the tools mentioned in this chapter, plus a few others. Each has its own approach for identifying investments with positive societal impact.

Another philosophy gaining in popularity is ESG investing, the letters standing for *environmental*, *social*, and *governance*. Integrated ESG analysis means incorporating ESG criteria when you examine the *financial* side of a company. There is no universal methodology for measuring E or S or G, however. Consider, for example, the E (environmental): We could ask things about a company such as whether it gets its energy from renewable sources, how well it recycles (or, better, if it embraces circular design), or whether it has dumped waste in the Hudson River and racked up fines with the EPA (same E).

PRI (Principles for Responsible Investment; an organization partnering with the United Nations) provides various illustrations of how ESG considerations might affect stock price: a car company's sales slowing on account of environmental concerns (stock price down); new environmental legislation imposing additional costs on a manufacturer (down); poor labor practices reducing productivity (down); or the diversity of a company's board of directors leading to lower borrowing costs (stock price up). By considering all relevant ESG factors — those posing risk or those offering opportunity — ESG analysis suggests that you can better predict which stocks will do well *financially*: it will be those that do "good." More and more we are learning this is true, though differences arise according to how things are measured.[95]

But how can *we* learn about companies using an ESG lens? You can look at a company's website, but it can be more useful to read sustainability reports. The GRI (Global Reporting Initiative) is a platform that has been used by major corporations since 1997 to report on their environmental and social sustainability. GRI reports were not specifically designed for investors but you can examine them to learn about companies' social and environmental behavior. There is an easy-to-use tool to view the GRI, and other, reports about corporate sustainability. (Don't forget to look at Appendix 6.)

Another approach to ESG investing but which involves less effort is to work with a financial advisory that has adopted PRI principles. PRI (the organization) has developed six Principles for Responsible Investment (or PRI principles). These commit financial institutions that advise about or sell stock (or other securities) to incorporate ESG into their financial analysis. Further, they are required to disclose their own ESG performance and to push the companies whose stock they promote to disclose theirs.[96] Over 3,000 financial firms have publicly adopted the PRI principles, and together they manage over $100 trillion. Some, but not all, of these firms publicly share their annual PRI reports.

But be clear: adopting an ESG focus is different from seeking to invest in companies trying their hardest to change the world. ESG is an attempt at more complete *financial* analysis — i.e., to make more money as an investor. Yet ESG criteria *do* align with inclusive opportunities; they do herald a shift to greener technology, fairer wages, and other socially beneficial outcomes. So a happy (and important) byproduct of incorporating ESG into financial analysis is taking a more thoughtful look at investing in companies that are taking strides to bring these changes about.

Many people forego investing in individual stocks and instead invest in a bundle of them: a mutual fund, an exchange traded fund (ETF), or an index fund. What is contained in these bundles is not up to you but up to the company that puts the bundle together. Every mutual fund or ETF uses a specific criterion to create its particular bundle. Examples: small company stocks, or overseas stocks, or stocks with long-term growth potential. An index fund bundles together an exceptionally large number of stocks that move exactly in sync with the overall stock market or some particular slice of it. Some funds, which can belong to any of these types, emphasize ESG criteria. That means you can invest in a bundle of stocks with high ESG scores.

Firms the like the financial research firm Morningstar can help you find ESG funds (it produces the Morningstar Sustainability Rating, available through its online ESG Screener). Other online tools help ESG investors as well, covering funds, individual stocks, and stock indices. The U.S. Department of Labor discusses over two dozen of them.

Many investors seek professional advice before investing. If you're in this situation, PRI advises you to ask a prospective stock adviser such questions as: What are your ESG integration practices? Do you have a dedicated ESG team? What ESG data, research, tools, practices, and resources do you use? (Additional questions can be found in Appendix 4.) You can, of course, ask a potential advisor if they subscribe to PRI principles.

ESG investing can also allow us to invest in the specific causes we care about. Some funds are theme-based, containing, say, only low-carbon stocks or stocks of companies with a strong record of gender equity. Some funds are also active in creating or supporting shareholder resolutions (voting issues) that try to force better corporate behavior. These might include: avoiding toxic chemicals; increasing diversity; or even forcing companies to disclose their ESG efforts more openly. You can own funds like these, lend them your "voice," and assign them your voting rights. That way, they represent lots of people at once. So, when they speak, corporations listen; and when they vote it makes a bigger difference. When you invest in a fund (or underlying firm) that is active with pro-social shareholder resolutions, you're supporting their actions.

Companies like the huge fossil fuel funder JPMorgan Chase often fight to prevent shareholders putting forward shareholder resolutions.[97] But their resistance only confirms the need for funds that will fight on our behalf, which is what ESG-related shareholder resolutions do.

True impact investing — at least as far as I'm concerned — emphasizes societal impact: impact *before* (even *in place of*) financial performance. Some people consider everything we've mentioned in this chapter so far to be impact investing. While I'm happy such options exist, and I see them as valuable, I believe there are other ways to invest which have greater impact.

So how do you invest to put impact truly front and center? Before I explain, first recognize two things: first, when we invest in stocks or mutual funds (or other funds or indices), we are really just shifting money around. I sell a company's stock and you buy it — at least in effect. The company does not receive new investment funds. And, second, that even picking a stock deemed acceptable according to ESG principles does not guarantee that it's from a company truly aiming to change the world. Even some oil and gas companies rate high on ESG scorecards.

So, as an alternative, you can make an investment that channels money directly to a company you believe will create societal impact by buying its "original" stock from it (this is very different from buying stock through, for example,

Charles Schwab or Robinhood). For instance, if you know someone who is starting a water distribution company in Uganda, you might buy stock (a piece of the company) directly from her. Your investment could also be in the form of a loan, where you get scheduled repayments but don't own a piece of the company. Investment opportunities like these are rare, however.

You may even find that social startups let you make unusual types of investments — a cross between buying a stock and making a loan. If you do happen upon any opportunity to invest in a social startup, make sure you've saved enough money already that you feel comfortable with the risk of making the investment. Most of us are not wealthy enough to *legally* invest in these companies anyway.

So ... what *can* we do to make genuine impact investments?

One approach became more accessible with the Jumpstart Our Business Startups (JOBS) Act, signed by President Obama, which opened the door to "investment crowdfunding," begun in 2016. This allows small businesses to sell stock or take loans from everyday people — and with limited effort and expense.

Investment crowdfunding is not what takes place on Kickstarter or Indiegogo, which promise rewards for donating money. Nor is it what occurs on sites like GoFundMe, which let you donate to a person, community, or a cause you care about, without getting your money back or receiving anything else in return. In contrast, *investment* crowdfunding (aka equity crowdfunding or regulation crowdfunding [Reg CF]) means you're investing in an actual business — not a project or campaign. You might make money; you might lose money. Investment crowdfunding is starting to take off, although it is minuscule compared to the activity on, say, the

New York Stock Exchange. Still, fewer than 20,000 people per month were crowdfunding investors in 2018, and now there are over 250,000.[98] In dollar terms, too, investment crowdfunding is growing. Wefunder, a large investment crowdfunding platform, currently helps investors invest more than $130 million a year, a volume that quadrupled from the year before.

In spring of 2021, new rules made it possible for existing businesses to raise larger crowdfunding investments each year, and for small businesses to "test the waters" (without cost) to see if investors are interested in investing in them. These new rules should accelerate the rise we already see in number of investors, dollar volume, and number of companies seeking crowdfunding investments.

Investment crowdfunding is attractive to both social entrepreneurs and local businesses. Traditional investors (venture capitalists) shy away from helping launch companies that have a social mission. Why, these investors think, would we want to support them if that reduces their focus on making money? But on investment crowdfunding platforms, these social enterprises can find investors who think like them. Netfunder, one such platform, offers three examples of companies finding investors on its site: a company bringing solar electricity to Africa, another supporting STEM education for girls and minorities, and a third that makes and distributes affordable wheelchairs around the world.[99] These companies have received between $200,000 and $1 million in investment each.

Small, local businesses are another beneficiary of crowdfunding investment, even when they are not startups. From previous chapters you'll recall the benefits that small, local businesses — the ones you can support as a customer — bring to a community. Businesses owned by women or

People of Color make up a larger fraction of businesses on investment crowdfunding platforms than elsewhere, and more than three-fourths of listed businesses receive the funding they're looking for. Over 30 crowdfunding platforms, with names like Wefunder, Crowdfund Mainstreet, and Netcapital, list small businesses seeking investors. They may be offering shares in their company or seeking loans. Investibule.co (not ".com") aggregates many of these platforms, so potential investors can see small businesses they might invest in in their own state or anywhere else across the country. Investment crowdfunding can help that restaurant you like which always has a wait, or support the organic farm whose market stall you try to visit before it sells out. Sometimes your eyes tell you the truth, but be aware that, like any investment, investment crowdfunding can be risky. Buying stock in a local business can be problematic because there is no stock market that lets you know a stock's "market price" when you buy it, or helps you sell it as soon as you want to.[100]

As with other kinds of stock, some funds bundle together the stock of local businesses, reducing an investor's risk of investing in any one of them. Though there are far, far fewer funds containing the stock of small, local businesses than there are ordinary mutual funds (which bundle stocks of major companies), they do exist. Many embrace a specific theme or geographic region. The organizations that offer these funds can be quite different from each other — some are for-profit, some are non-profit; some are loan funds, some are stock funds; some pay you back according the financial performance of the underlying "portfolio companies," and some do not. A report co-authored by the National Coalition for Community Capital lists examples of these types of funds as well as the steps to take to create one.[101]

Some of these funds have been around for a while. Since the mid-1980s, RSF Social Finance has been thinking about how the economy should operate to serve people and the planet and the role finance can play in changing it. One of the things I was struck by when I studied RSF for my last book[102] was how it brings together business borrowers and lenders to discuss what interest rates borrowers should pay — and lenders (investors) should receive — when a loan is made. This discussion, which sets for three months what RSF calls the RSF-prime interest rate, underlies RSF's Social Investment Fund. The Social Investment Fund invests exclusively in "mission first" social enterprises. You can live in 49 of the 50 states (I don't know which the anomaly is) and invest in this fund if you are able to invest at least $1,000. RSF offers other funds only to accredited (wealthy) investors and foundations, and these require a minimum investment 100 times as large.

At the first RSF price-setting meeting after Covid-19 hit the United States, borrowers (businesses) explained how risky and uncertain everything had become due to Covid as lenders (investors) listened. If there ever was a similar meeting between small businesses and *conventional* lenders, the conversation might have gone like this: "As investors making you a loan, we agree things have become very risky for you and that your business is in uncharted territory. But that makes any loan we make more risky for *us* because we might not get repaid. So we insist that interest rates should be set *higher*." At RSF, the real conversation went exactly the opposite way, with investors recognizing the new risk that these business were now facing, and then suggesting borrowers' interest rates be *lowered* to make the business's financial lives easier. As a result, borrowers saw their rates go down, and RSF also set up a fund to help borrowers struggling to repay their loans.[103]

I recently learned something that may be even more surprising about the way RSF is trying to transform the financial system: now, when anyone receives a loan, a legal covenant in the loan agreement says that the borrower, along with RSF, will do 21 days of kindness.[104] A financial company spreading kindness by reimaging their lending.

Strong *place*-based funds sometimes arise organically as a piece of a larger ecosystem of "collective action." A recent effort, the Boston Ujima Project, is creating an economy to support Boston's working class. It seeks a working class with better access to housing, food, jobs, and other necessities. One part of the Ujima Project is the Boston Ujima Fund. The fund receives capital from local citizens, civic organizations, social activists, and others, which is then invested to support local businesses and other civic needs. Decisions about what to invest in are made by community members affected by those decisions. The Ujima Project offers investees business skills training and arranges institutional purchasing from them. It also certifies the businesses it invests in according to standards set by Ujima's voting members. These include: providing livable wages; supporting the safety and wellbeing of workers and their families; and giving voice to workers at their places of work. The Ujima Fund offers a variety of investment options — some only available to Massachusetts residents, who may invest any amount from $50. Other options are available for wealthier (accredited) individuals. Though the fund carries risk, its rules state that ordinary (non-accredited) investors get the best rate of return and will be the first to be repaid if the fund suffers a loss.

We are early in the history of local investment and funds like the Ujima Fund. To commit to — and invest in — a place you care about, they represent a promising option.

Takeaways from this chapter

Unless you are very wealthy, the best you can probably do with your investment dollars if you want to "do good" is to buy stocks that have high ESG ratings. These ratings don't mean the company is always striving to do good, but more likely that they're trying to avoid a hit to their stock price as a result of doing bad. One other way to invest to "do good": you can invest in local businesses and social enterprises, using new types of investment, to create jobs and grow communities.

10 DON'T EAT BREAKFAST

In the age of a pandemic, civil unrest, and escalating threats to democracy, the climate crisis remains the most dire problem of our times.

Writing in the *New Yorker* magazine, Jonathan Franzen put it plainly: "There is no hope, except for us."[105] The article is a plea for us to start thinking seriously about a future where climate destruction has made the world a Hollywood-esque dystopia, and stop thinking only about what is more immediate or more pleasant. "Every day," when we wake up, Franzen writes, "instead of thinking about breakfast, [we] have to think about death."

That is our hope. To recognize a future so bleak that we don't arrive there.

There is an urgent need to institute huge structural changes — things only governments can do, such as: imposing massive costs on business activities that produce carbon dioxide (CO_2); or, more effectively, creating a regulatory framework in which it is impossible to profit from carbon-producing activities — if we are to stop the worst effects of an overheating planet.

But what can any one of *us* do? While system-level change is necessary and urgent to mitigate the worst of the looming catastrophes, we can each make a commitment to be less part of the problem and more part of the solution. As we now know from the previous chapters focusing on our financial behavior, we should never underestimate the potential of aggregated individual actions, nor the value of "being the change." The transformative (and mysterious) power of "emergence" will be explored in the next chapter.

We can make adjustments to our transportation habits (fly less, drive less, and use public transportation). Eat less meat (to reduce methane emissions and stall the environmentally damaging incursions of huge agribusinesses). Avoid food waste. Buy less, and recycle more. Reduce our use of heat, power, and water (adjust our thermostats, limit conveniences like air conditioning, and take shorter showers). Reduce packaging (use personal shopping bags). Shop at farmers' markets (to reduce food transportation). And try to bundle your online purchases into fewer shipments (similarly, try to plan your real-world shopping so you get everything in one trip).

Yet the big question at our breakfast tables should be: What changes in behavior can we make that would have the *greatest effect* on the climate, especially considering only a small number of us are ever likely to make them?

The Center for Behavior & the Environment (CBE; part of the non-profit Rare.org) and California Environmental Associates (CEA) raised this very question. To answer it, they began with dozens of solutions developed by Project Drawdown to curtail the rise in the greenhouse gases[106] that have caused the climate crisis. Using this list, CBE and CEA sought any changes in *consumer* behavior the impacts of which would be significant were only 10% of us to make them. To qualify, these behavioral changes also had to be feasible, with neither price, inconvenience, nor stigma representing barriers. And there must be enough people realistically able to make the change to permit a 10% adoption target (Center for Behavior & the Environment 2019).[107]

In this way, CBE and CEA identified seven changes the combined effects of which would be to close 80% of the U.S.'s CO_2 commitment gap: that is, the gap between (a) the amount of CO_2 (or greenhouse gas equivalents) the U.S. is predicted to emit by 2025 based on our current pattern of emissions (having only recently rejoined the Paris Climate Agreement) and (b) what our emissions would have amounted to had we fully complied with that commitment. In numbers, that gap has been calculated at 600 million metric tons. So those seven changes in behavior — undertaken by only 10% of us with no individual expected to make all seven changes — would shrink that gap by a massive 500 million tons.

The CBE–CEA report concludes that, "without making dramatic lifestyle changes and in the absence of sweeping new policies, a small portion of Americans can have a measurable, substantive impact on reducing national emissions." It highlights three behavioral changes that would have by far the greatest impact. If 10% of car buyers bought an electric vehicle — 1.3 million new purchases — it would put a noticeable dent in our voracious consumption of gasoline and eliminate 65 million tons of CO_2 per year. It would also save nearly $800 in cash per year for drivers who switch, and create social benefits estimated to be between $3 and $33 billion annually.[108]

A similar result would derive from the use of solar energy for heating and cooling, lighting, cooking, and powering appliances — instead of energy generated from fossil fuel. This change would close the gap by another 60 million tons or so, with an annual social benefit of between $4 and $40 billion. Fewer than 12 million households would have to change their behavior to make this a reality.

Other changes would produce more modest impacts (though they are still important given the urgency of the problem), and they include: eating more plants and less meat (which is *not* to say becoming 100% vegetarian, which is a step too far for many) and reducing food waste. Substituting teleconferencing for air travel will make a modest difference as well.

But the greatest impact in reducing emissions of CO_2, according to CBE and CEA, would come from something very few of us are doing: offsetting our personal carbon. The impact could be so great that it is worth our while to understand it.

Each of us has a carbon footprint: the amount of CO_2 attributable to us by our choices and actions (for convenience, this is often simply referred to as "carbon"). Flying puts CO_2 in the skies, a portion of which can be assigned to each passenger. So does eating meat (which produces more CO_2 than a plant-based diet), driving a car, running appliances, etc. Just as we can increase our physical activity with the aim of making the calories we burn equal to the calories we ingest, we can offset our personal carbon output by taking a counterbalancing action. We might plant trees (which capture CO_2), but who has the time or a spare acre? And how many would we need to plant to compensate for driving a 30-mile round trip to work each day or taking a flight from New York to New Orleans?

But tools are available to help us negate our carbon. Some tell us how much carbon we're responsible for; others help us offset it — whether that's at an event level, such as a vacation or business travel, or at the level of your entire lifestyle. See Appendix 7.

CO_2 can be bought and sold via two types of transactions, both of which aim to reduce the amount entering the atmosphere. (1) Companies that dramatically reduce their emissions may seek credit for this. In a cap-and-trade system, which is one example, a company is given a limit on how much CO_2 it can produce. If it's exceeding that limit, it would be forced to invest in new technology or adopt new practices to keep below it. But if it produces less, it now has something to sell. A firm like the first (the one producing more than it was supposed to) can buy the second firm's excess "good behavior" to count as its own — for the going price. What is sold is, conveniently, called a carbon credit (or permit), and it is traded on a carbon market. A carbon credit is associated with 1 metric ton of carbon reduced or avoided. Mandatory carbon markets (also called compliance markets) exist where regulations have created them, which can be done by a city, state, region, country, or even something as expansive as the European Union. Companies emit less carbon when the price of credits becomes sufficiently expensive that it's better to curtail their own emissions than to purchase credits.

The other way in which CO_2 is sold is *à la carte*, which can happen when an environmental project takes CO_2 out of the air or avoids putting it there in the first place. Planting trees is one of the best examples of the first type of project. Via photosynthesis, a tree absorbs CO_2, does some chemistry to store it as wood, and creates oxygen to boot. A tree's downside is it takes years to grow, it might not survive, it may be cut down, and you need lots of land to grow them. (This, naturally, leads to complications in measuring the good that derives from planting a tree.)

An example of a project that avoids the future release of CO_2, rather than actually taking it out of the air, is selling (or donating) solar cookers so that people don't have to burn kerosene to boil water or cook. A non-profit might run a solar cooker project in Peru, allowing people to replace dirty, expensive kerosene with clean solar. Most importantly for our purposes: if the amount of kerosene that was not burnt can be accurately quantified (which translates into CO_2 avoided), the project can sell that as a carbon "offset." That purchaser could be anyone, including you or me. Offsets from projects like these are sold on voluntary carbon markets, not the mandatory markets where credits are traded. Forestry and land use projects amount to nearly 50% of the monetary value of voluntary carbon markets, which is more than 2.5 times that of renewables, the next largest category.[109]

Around the world, companies are beginning to get the hang of buying and selling carbon credits — not least because, in many places, it is now a requirement. The European Union Emissions Trading System (EU ETS), a cap-and-trade system in which high-polluting industries must participate, is Europe's key policy tool for holding down the emissions of greenhouse gases and is the world's largest carbon market. Cap and trade works only when the price of carbon credits becomes so expensive that it deters polluting companies from just buying credits from other firms to stay within compliance. The EU ETS has been restricting the supply of credits to drive up their price, which has topped $100 per ton and could be twice that by the end of the decade.[110] The value of global carbon markets now stands at over $800 billion.[111]

A much smaller volume of activity takes place on voluntary, rather than compliance, carbon markets, on which carbon offsets are bought and sold. The world voluntary carbon market is, at most, 1% the size of the compliance market. Still, it traded more than $1 billion in offsets last year, more than tripling in two years.[112] Projects that produce carbon offsets originate in many diverse locations worldwide, often taking advantage of a country's natural features: its sunlight, wind, or good soil for planting and growing trees, for example. The cost of buying these offsets varies a great deal across projects. Yet these voluntary markets may unlock a future in which there is a price (penalty) to pay for producing planet-destroying CO_2. These markets are more readily established than compliance markets, which must be underpinned by new laws; as such, they are capable of providing a wealth of timely data about new projects that can be useful in avoiding carbon or sequestering (capturing) it.[113]

The important point here is that *individuals* can buy offsets on voluntary carbon markets,[114] a fact that should appeal to anyone who wants to play a part in protecting the planet. Carbon projects on voluntary markets often come with other desirable features that will appeal to the same buyers; for example, some emphasize creation of new jobs, others provision of new skills, or public health benefits. For instance, water filters, brought in as a substitute for boiling the water by burning wood, can thereby lead to improvements in indoor air quality and a fall in respiratory diseases. Some estimates equate such "social" benefits to $100 per ton of carbon.[115]

If you want to know how much carbon you are personally responsible for in your daily life, carbon calculators are available. For instance, according to one calculator, my driving emits about three tons of carbon in a year. To offset this amount, I can spend between $30 and $50 to purchase carbon offsets — choosing among, for example, wind farms in China, cook stoves in India, or tree planting in the United Kingdom. To offset all the carbon associated with my lifestyle, I can add in the amount of carbon I'm responsible for at home (heating and cooling, cooking, electricity use) and when I drive or fly, and even the carbon I'm only indirectly responsible for (because of the clothes I buy or the TV shows I watch — none of which come "carbon-free"). Having calculated the totality of the carbon I'm responsible for, I get my personal carbon footprint. But how great an impact could individuals have if we acted to offset our carbon?

Today, few of us buy carbon offsets, despite their potential to mitigate the climate crisis. CBE and CEA explain that we could eliminate nearly *half* the emissions we are committed to reducing under the Paris Climate Agreement if just 5% of us offset our personal carbon footprint — which means only 17 million people out of a U.S. population of 330 million shouldering some blame for the unfolding climate crisis and taking responsibility for it.[116] The 5% goal (in contrast to the 10% participation rate chosen for other behavioral changes) acknowledges not only that individual participation in voluntary carbon markets is currently low but also that few people even know it's an option. CBE and CEA add that, on top of the climate benefits, hitting the 5% mark would also produce societal benefits estimated at between $12 and $142 billion.

Critics of carbon offsets warn about the difficulties in measurement. If you plant a tree, it won't store an appreciable amount of carbon for years — so at what point can that planting generate an offset that can be sold? What if the tree is counted twice? What if it is inadvertently logged? What if . . . Other critics voice more profound concerns: this approach is just buying our way out of bad behavior, and it is inconsistent with the ultimate goal of dramatically reducing the carbon in the atmosphere. And that relying on carbon markets reinforces the idea that markets can fix all ills, when capitalism itself is seen as the core problem.

But, despite these concerns, time is running out. And there is much that we can do right away. The most responsible course of action is, *first*, to reduce our carbon footprints as much as we can; then, after we've done all we can in that regard, purchase offsets to do even more. Paying for the damage we do is worthwhile, but purchasing offsets should be done *in addition to* — not instead of — reducing our emissions. Reducing carbon in absolute terms — rather than adding here, subtracting there in equal measure — must be the aim.

This argument applies even more to corporations than to us. And we have roles we can play here, too. Environmental activist-author Bill McKibben has been working to build the climate movement for over three decades, founding the leading climate campaign organization, 350.org. He notes the dramatic drop in the price of solar and wind energy, which required large subsidies only recently before dropping 90% in the last decade and very soon becoming cheaper than fossil fuels — nearly everywhere.[117] Already, using existing solar and wind technology and available land, we could produce *one hundred times* the *world's energy needs*. This would result in trillions of dollars saved by energy consumers, not counting the benefits that accrue to the planet.[118]

McKibben is encouraged that everyday actions are visibly chipping away at fossil fuel behemoths: "[E]very time a new electric [heat pump] is installed, the wealth — and hence the political power of the fossil-fuel industry — declines a tick further, in the kind of virtuous cycle that we badly need to keep accelerating. Hail the humble heat pump."[119] Within the investment community, there is dawning awareness that fossil-based fuels make bad investments.

What must occur now, McKibben explains, is a concerted push to "tip" the system to renewable energy, since the unholy alliance of the fossil fuel industry, their bankers, and the politicians they support financially will resist the transition away from fossil as forcefully as they can. Yet McKibben is encouraged by the growth of the anti-fossil fuel social movement, which includes divestments, protests, boycotts, voting, and even getting in "good trouble" (getting arrested). "If those keep growing . . . ," he explains, "we may be able to push our politicians and our banks hard enough that they actually let us benefit from the remarkable fall in the price of renewable energy. . . . [Activists and engineers together] offer the only hope of even beginning to catch up with the runaway pace of global warming."[120]

Buying offsets to compensate for your whole lifestyle will seem like a daunting challenge to many. So let us remember our 15% approach introduced in Chapter 1. Target one aspect of your life and make it carbon-neutral (which is simply a way of saying that the offsets you buy or create are equal to the emissions you're responsible for). That aspect could be all your personal travel (or just your flights). Or maybe a wedding or a big event you're going to throw.

As a 16-year-old, Greta Thunberg sailed across the Atlantic in 2019 to attend the United Nations Climate Action Summit . The face of youthful climate activism,[121] she sent an open letter to every EU leader and head of state (having collected over 10,000 signatures — a number currently standing at over 125,000), pleading: "You must stop pretending that we can solve the climate and ecological crisis without treating it as a crisis."[122]

There is so much to do, but also so many ways we can play our part.

What seems like it will take forever can also change in an instant.

Takeaways from this chapter

You may feel overwhelmed — many of us do. But a focus on what we can do for the environment *right now* is drastically needed. We can make a difference. But we must wake up and stop sleepwalking. A strong option available to each of us is to offset the carbon associated with our lives.

11 $1+1+1+$ $\ldots = ?$

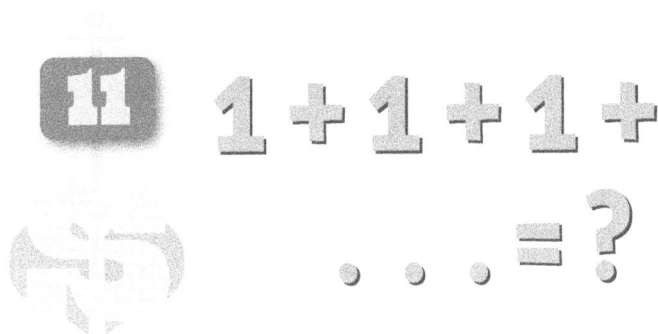

Why should you do good with your money when it seems other people aren't? Will it even make a difference?

Here I want to make the point that large shifts in the world can be *emergent*. One aspect of *emergence* is that what occurs in an outwardly visible way is due to activity beneath the surface that doesn't appear to predict or explain it. Keeping this point in mind is useful in considering what our actions *might* achieve, even if we don't see results right away, or even after what seems like a long time.

This chapter presents some ideas about emergence, and I invite you to explore them with curiosity. They are my attempt to describe a mosaic in which each of us lives a tiny life (when measured against the sum total of the actions of everyone on the planet, plus all of history that has preceded us), and yet in which somehow things change and what we do matters. It may appear we have no power. But we might be molecules in a spinning tornado of change that binds us together into something powerful. While this chapter is not specifically about money, it is about change. As such, its lessons apply to everything else we've already looked at.

But, before we turn to emergence, let's acknowledge something: sometimes, there *are* clear causal chains linking actions to impact. As an example, if you're concerned about animal welfare you can change your eating habits. For every egg you don't eat, 0.91 fewer eggs are produced; for each pound of pork you avoid, production is decreased by 0.74 pounds. This is because, even though most times your decision to avoid these foods won't make a difference, sometimes many people make similar decisions at once; and, on those occasions, your grocer might end up buying a hundred pounds less pork, or several fewer cases of eggs — which translates into fewer animals raised for our consumption. So, even if you don't make a difference *every time* you make a pro-animal welfare choice, if you continue to make such choices, you *are* improving the lives of animals *on average*.[123]

Maybe you see this as "the little stuff." But remember: the actions of a small percentage among us can add up in large — and predictable — ways. As we've seen in Chapter 10, the actions of 10% of us can make a big difference in protecting the environment. With that in mind, let's now take a look my explanation of *emergence*.

1. What happens at one "level" of a system is different than what happens at another

Example. In the 1970s, a series of now well-known studies explored what would happen if Black families and White families moved to homes in new locations based solely on a rule about the race of their current neighbors.[124] To simulate this behavior, markers of two colors (black and white) are randomly placed on the squares of a large, two-dimensional grid (any square is either empty or has one marker on it). Each marker can "see" what percentage of its occupied "neighbors" (the eight squares that surround it) are markers its own color. If (and only if) the percentage is below a specified threshold, the marker moves to the nearest unoccupied square where the percentage of like-colored neighbors is high enough. Every marker applies this same rule, again and again, until an overall pattern stabilizes.

So what happens when the threshold is set at 20%? This implies that each marker is "happy" (and won't move) so long as at least 20% of its neighbors share its color. In real life, such families would be considered racially tolerant, content to live among a majority (up to 80%) of families of another race. In the simulation, some markers will need to move to satisfy this rule, but the overall pattern that emerges after things settle down is a random distribution of black and white markers across the board.

Now suppose the threshold is 33% — meaning that a black marker requires one-third of its neighbors to be black to stay put (and the reverse for white markers). In this instance (which in real life would still describe racially tolerant families), the overall pattern that emerges is no longer a random distribution of black and white markers but 80% "segregated" (where segregation means a blob of all one color made up of contiguous markers). What is going on here? Each family is making a personal ("micro") decision about its behavior. But the *interactions* among them produces "macro" (neighborhood) effects. A relatively small shift in *personal* thresholds from 20% to 33% (both of which are conceived as "racially tolerant") creates a qualitative difference in whether a *neighborhood* is integrated or segregated.[125]

What has emerged is a "whole" with properties of its own, not of its parts. Both the thresholds under investigation describe situations in which every family welcomes integration. But a 33% threshold precludes it at a neighborhood level.

Few of us would predict that segregation could be caused by such a simple rule, even in a simulation. Or that individual preferences when added together would look so different at a community level. Or that a small change in the threshold could make so much difference. *That* is the essence of emergence: it surprises. "Macro" effects arise from "micro" actions in mysterious ways.

2. A long period of stability may give rise to one of rapid change

Example. An ant colony suddenly switches its preference from one food source to another, even though it has consistently gotten food from the first source and the new source is not better in any way (this actually happens). A model of this behavior shows how the actions of a tiny number of individuals can dramatically shift the behavior of a much larger group. Once in a great while, to start with, a single ant strikes out in a new direction to find food. This single *deviation* can begin a cascade in which hundreds or thousands of other ants also adjust their behavior — even abandoning a perfectly good food source for a new one — without any instructions from the queen or another authority coordinating their behavior.

Yet the colony's behavior will "tip" due to the behavior of a few, ordinary ants.

A simple explanation for this dramatic shift is that the first ant's deviant behavior is noticed and imitated, then another imitates that, and so on — until each ant adopts it, and so does the colony. Mathematically[126] — although all the actual math is hidden here — here's what's going on. Ants are creatures of habit, and each ant usually returns to where it got food the last time. But, once in a while, an ant simply wanders off in a new direction, sometimes following a chemical trail laid down by a recently returning ant (no matter which food source that ant was returning from). When these rare events occur in the right order and in sufficient numbers, one right after the other, the entire colony will abandon one food source for another.

But deviance doesn't guarantee followers: other ants *may* follow a deviant's behavior, but much more often they don't. Eventually, a deviation gains momentum, however, and then there is no stopping it. Until then, for a long period, the colony dines at the first source. But when the colony's behavior has tipped, the second source becomes the norm and stays that way until similar behavior again tips it in another direction.

We can see swings like this in our preferences for technology, fashion, societal issues, and much more. Individuals are involved, but it is the interactions among us that cause a dramatic systemic shift. It is just as hard to explain *why* these shifts are happening as it is to predict *when* they will occur. For instance, in 2001, adults in the U.S. opposed same-sex marriage in a 2:1 ratio. By 2017, the ratio was reversed. (Marriage equality became law in 2015.) The system tipped, yet no one had predicted it. Even now, no one, not even sociologists, can really explain it. The Stonewall Riots in Greenwich

Village in 1969, and countless laws and court cases over the ensuing decades, all played a role; but none of these was the cause. Each might seem like a small pebble being added to one side of a see-saw until a child sitting at the other end finally lifts off the ground; but, in that analogy, physics tells us that the shift is inevitable, whereas when it came to marriage equality you could never say, "only 15 more pebbles to go." There was no way of telling which pebble was going to tilt the balance and change millions of lives.

Moving on from describing emergence in terms of mathematical abstractions, we now turn to the roles that people play in it.

3. Certain people sense what is emerging; others join them

The foregoing may imply a sense of powerlessness in the face of forces outside our control — as if we are H_2O molecules, dependent on temperature to determine whether we are water or ice. But that doesn't seem right, at least not to me. To stick with the analogy, maybe we can sense the heat starting to rise and recognize our opportunity to become steam.

Example. Ruth Bader Ginsburg was a pioneering crusader for women's rights. When she entered Harvard Law School in 1956, she was one of only nine females among the school's 500 students.[127] The dean let them know they were taking slots away from men. When she graduated, top of her class (from Columbia; she transferred for personal reasons), she was recommended by a Harvard law professor to clerk for Supreme Court Justice Felix Frankfurter. He demurred:

he preferred a man. Then-common occurrences like these informed her legal perspective.

Before joining the Supreme Court, she had worked on both the theory and practice of promoting women's rights, including founding the ACLU's Women's Rights Project. In the 1970s, she argued five cases before the Court. At the time, the 14th Amendment to the U.S. Constitution was distant history, having been adopted shortly after the Civil War. The Amendment's Equal Protection clause stated that newly freed slaves should receive the same protections under the law as White people. That was a different era: women were considered the property of their husbands; they could not own property themselves; and they could not vote. Yet Ginsburg recognized that the ideas that applied to newly freed slaves — equality under the law — applied just as surely when she was arguing cases before the Court with regard to gender. She argued that women should be treated no less favorably than men, and men should be treated no less favorably than woman. She developed this concept in her work at the ACLU, where she was involved in 34 cases before the Court, arguing six herself and winning five of them. The issues at stake were technical matters, such as: could a woman be the executor of her son's estate when her ex-husband wanted to be? and Should a man get housing and medical benefits (like a woman would) when his wife declares him her dependent? By choosing cases like these to argue, and with an ability to translate the decisions made in the aftermath of the Civil War to a contemporary context, Ruth Bader Ginsburg helped usher in a new era of gender-based equality and women's rights.

We can now see a "through-line" in all this: the arrow of time threading through events — beginning in the past, poised in her present, and reaching into the future. Of course, she didn't know and couldn't control how events would unfold while she was in the midst of her work; those outcomes represented a future she could only sense but one which she wanted to bring about: a more just society, especially for women. She couldn't have dared imagine that, when she died, about half of all law students and 30% of law school deans would be women. Or that she herself would serve on the Supreme Court with two other female justices (the number of female justices, from the date of the Court's founding until 1980, was . . . zero).[128]

Others before her had unsuccessfully pursued a similar agenda, even with great legal skill. But it was RBG's deviance that finally helped pull us all into the future. But so did the women, men, and children she influenced, who in turn influenced others — they all played vital a role as well. Positive deviance always requires followers if it is to create an impact.[129]

Behavior arising from the connections among us is the heart of human system change, no matter how unpredictable or surprising it might be. Even without any formal planning, organizing, or directing, one individual's actions can attract those of others, like a growing snowball. And — but only once in a great while — that individual may be as talented, and ultimately famous, as Ruth Bader Ginsburg. There is a special role for those who notice the deviator, and support or adopt her practices. Without these "fast followers," there is no snowball. Every one of us influences others.

4. Context can encourage large shifts (in behavior, norms, attitudes, or expectations)

Example. Among the medical problems endured on the African continent are:

1. African students who train to become doctors often get their training abroad; when they graduate, two things often keep them from returning home: either a "life event" (say, marriage to someone from the U.S.) or an "opportunity" (to earn higher wages by staying abroad).

2. Related to point (1), relative to other parts of the world there is an incredibly short supply of neonatal physicians and healthcare workers. This shortage causes preventable deaths among newborns and children.

Recent investments, however, have led to the training of African pediatric and neonatal specialists — in Africa, by African doctors — resulting in 98% of these physicians remaining in their home country.[130]

In this example, investment has created a *context* in which a pattern of events can unfold. Most obviously, newborns and children should be healthier as a result. But this might also end up applying to their mothers, families, and their communities. When neonatal specialists and pediatricians are trained and retained at home, this can build a health infrastructure that grows to encompass more areas of specialized care and which will serve more people.

After an investment in neonatal/pediatric training, some people might try to forecast what will happen. Others might invest, based on those forecasts. Ask yourself: are these forecasters "hastening" the future by attracting investors? How could we ever know the ultimate results of these forecasts? Which stones tossed in a pond cause enduring ripples, and how do all these ripples interact? The effects of doctors training at home and staying there may be felt for generations. But exactly *how*? That remains to be determined.

Establishing a context for change is not a recipe for change. But an enabling context can unite individuals in ways in which one another's energy and intention combine in ways that could not have been predicted, until all bursts forth as a flower in a field, or maybe becomes a forest.

Takeaways from this chapter

How does societal change occur? I don't know, but I suggest it might be close to this: At the right time, there is a wave. It is both propelling us forward (as if we were surfing) but we're incrementally pulling it ahead, too. If the right surfer comes along, or enough of us start to surf, we may transform small waves into larger waves. Note: I don't surf, but in this chapter I do write about *emergence*, and the *tl;dr* version looks like this:

1. The segregated checkerboards. There can be simple, interacting rules (activities) that produce a (surprising) result, even if we don't "see" them at play "under the surface."

2. The ants' food source. Patterns may seem "fixed" until, suddenly, a whole "colony" shifts based on a few rare events occurring in particular combinations.

3. Ruth Bader Ginsburg. The focus of individuals on what they sense as emerging is important; and they must be joined or followed by others to have effect.

4. African neonatal healthcare. We can create a context that leads to change even though we are unable to control the outcome.

"Doing good with money" can exhibit emergent behavior like this. What we do *can* make a difference.

Note: the Postscript, "The Future We Create," shows the dramatic shifts the United States has experienced with respect to the purpose and responsibilities of business. It may surprise you!

12 MEDITATION ON MY OWN BOOK

I'm going to recap the ideas in this book differently than I've presented them — examining them as if they were an onion, so to speak.

On the exterior of this onion, on its papery dried leaves, is everything we *observe*. With respect to money, this includes such things as: what we buy, the prices we pay, jobs that are created or lost, and a host of formal measures — Gross National Product or Gross National Happiness Index (which the country of Bhutan uses instead), and measures of economic inequality. This, of course, is only the tiniest glimpse of what we can observe.

We can also see a world full of fears and uncertainty: a pandemic, a climate (planetary) crisis, the threat of autocracy, wars and murders, and indignities including hundreds of millions of people not having enough to eat, a place to sleep, or being treated "less than" by society. We have noted the connections between these things and money.

Can we explain how these observations come about?

Below the surface of this onion is the vast *machinery* that cranks out what we observe. This machinery includes our businesses, our institutions, our laws, rules we are expected to follow, our systems of communication . . . In fact, *systems* or *structures* are more precise terms than "machinery," if we understand them to mean not *what* we observe in the world but *how* it has come about.

One of these systems is the system of money. It is a potent system in the way it directs resources and captures our attention, and because its tentacles seem to reach everywhere. Within the system of money, we are actors — we "finance" certain outcomes. By that I mean: "we allow to happen." When we buy a particular item, we allow that product to "happen." If no one bought it, it wouldn't be made. Our banking choices, as a second example, either finance home lending where we live, or contribute to our money being whisked away to be used elsewhere.

This characterization can help us see the many ways *we* bring about the world we live in. We, as individuals. We, as communities. We, who feel ourselves a part of something larger. As financial actors we earn, buy, save, invest, give money away. Those actions affect health, education, economics, civil rights, human rights, and our planet.

With the world heading toward its four billionth birthday, we have arrived at this moment. It's easy to forget that we have brought ourselves here. Somehow, and collectively, through the systems and structures *we* have built, which produce all we see before us.

Beneath this set of financial mechanisms lie our *beliefs* (which are closely associated with our thoughts and feelings about things) — the next layer of the onion.

Consider this "foundational" rule of business economics: a business should always try to make as much money as it can with as little cost to itself. Some of us are taught this; or we accept a version of it simply as the way things are. Or maybe we are fearful that we won't have enough ourselves, so this rule reinforces our own ideas about how we should behave. Yet this rule is simply a belief.

Or consider this: the rate of Black homeownership is lower than that of Whites (an accurate observation). One reason stems from banks' use of redlining decades ago to exclude Blacks from obtaining home mortgages in certain neighborhoods (a systematic rule enforced by the banking system). Ideas used to justify that system were that Whites and Blacks don't mix; or that Black people are less deserving. Like the idea that businesses should exclusively (or primarily) look out for themselves, these, too, are beliefs — thoughts about how the world works, thoughts about what (or who) is right and wrong, good and bad, etc. etc.

Our beliefs lie at a deep layer of the onion. And they give rise to structures and systems, which themselves give rise to what we observe (good and bad). Our beliefs have consequences.

Yet, as we can easily tell, beliefs are not absolute. People used to think the world was flat. Legally, women used to be their husband's property. We (or at least the physicists among us) now explain that two subatomic particles can perfectly mirror each other's actions, *simultaneously* (no delay!), even when separated by extreme distances. That's weird, right? So it can humble us into recognizing that what we believe is simply our own personal stew of ideas — unlike anyone else's, at least in all the details — and far from complete or accurate. Of course, our differences are also on display when we talk with friends or relatives, or sit down to watch the news.

With clashing beliefs, and beliefs feeding systems, and systems churning out observable outcomes, how can we hope for a kinder, more inclusive world? What might generate ideas leading to that world?

Here, our values come in. You may feel safer carrying a gun; I'd prefer a world without any guns. We have different beliefs about guns. But we both *value* safety. That is common ground. Or you may have a deep connection with nature, while my deepest connection is with my family or community. But we recognize in each other how important the *value* of connection is.

As we begin to see ourselves as "the same," we begin to see the world differently. We feel invited to be kinder, more generous, available to serve and to support others. We look for solutions that meet everyone's needs; we begin to see ourselves as part of all of life. This is the core of the onion.

In terms of doing good with money, seeing and valuing each other as "the same" can lead to the following kinds of beliefs. Rules should be fair for everyone. The goal should be for everyone to have enough. Money is simply a tool, to be used as we choose. There are values much more important than earning money. There are ways to live deep, fulfilling lives that don't make money the object.

Built on these kinds of beliefs, different kinds of systems/ structures arise; for instance:

- The belief that everyone should be treated fairly underlies CDFIs (which provide banking services to un-/underserved communities).

- The idea that business can become an experiment in generosity underlies Karma Kitchen, where your meal has already been paid for and you pay for someone you will never know.

- The idea that we should treat each other as neighbors underlies Everytable. Everytable offers affordable, nutritious, fresh food throughout Los Angeles. It prepares all meals in a central kitchen and then charges different prices in different neighborhoods for the same items, according to how much people can afford. (In essence, wealthy neighbors pay a little more so that their less wealthy neighbors can pay prices affordable to them.)

These, like many other examples, show how values such as kindness, generosity, and compassion can spark more inclusive and caring behavior.

And that's good news.

If we look, we might see an emerging pattern of thought that points the way out of troubling times, towards something better. The thorough disruption caused by a corona virus (less than a billionth our size) revealed our vulnerability as a species but also opened eyes, and hearts, to the idea that we may be on the verge of something else: something simpler but more authentic; more inclusive, embracing a much wider definition of what is "of value." Value connected to community, caring, and generosity.

At the heart of this is a respect for nature — and all of life. The climate crisis will not be forgiving. We can imagine the planet becoming violently less habitable, *or* us pulling together for the planet and society. We will all play some part in either outcome. And, if we pay attention, nature offers countless lessons about living and the continuity and interconnectedness of life.

Thus, at the heart of "doing good with money" is wisdom. Something that might resonate in us all, if we let it. Something timeless, welcoming. Something helping us sense what's needed, to bring it forward. How we view the planet, our neighbors, and future generations — big questions we can choose to examine — either sustain the patterns we see *or* set in motion something new. The wisdom we require is not a matter of books and better information (though those can be useful), but comes from what connects us, what fills our hearts. Coming from that place, our thoughts and beliefs, our decisions and actions, the rules that guide us, and systems we build — the world — are all open for change.

Takeaways from this chapter

We can observe all manner of strife and suffering in the world. But, at a deep place, we can find interconnection — with nature and each other. We all share the same fundamental needs: to be understood, to feel safe, to feel belonging. And, when we get in touch with these values, we open to beliefs that are inclusive rather than restrictive; compassionate rather than cut-throat. We begin to move from "me" (the ends justify the means; business should make as much money as possible; some people are "worth" more than others, . . .) to "we" (our fates our intertwined; all life has equal value; nature is priceless; . . .); and from there to building a world embodying love and abundance, rather than fear and scarcity. The ripples from these changes may result in a world now barely imaginable.

THE FUTURE WE CREATE

We are living in an age in which corporations wield huge power within our society. It seems like, in the U.S., it might always have been like this. Is that true? The answer is: no. Getting to this point involved a slow creep. I've chosen three snapshots of America which show just how much corporate behavior and responsibilities have changed over the course of our history. The fourth snapshot suggests what we might become again.

Snapshot A: Founding

Once, American corporations unquestionably had the public interest in mind. This was partly a reaction to British corporations' attitude toward the New World: they saw it as little more than a land to explore, somewhere to extract wealth from, and a population to sell goods to. Chartered by the Crown, they could harvest natural resources, such as lumber, for free; and, like other colonies, colonial America would be a new market for goods, such as furniture, made back in Britain. Some corporations, the East India Company being the most powerful and famous example, were given monopoly rights in the colonies.

The newly formed United States wanted something else from its corporations. After all, corporations (it is often forgotten) were initially established by governments to perform specific, limited tasks for the betterment of its citizens — tasks the government could not undertake itself. So the first American corporations were granted charters for projects such as building and operating a bridge, a canal, a port, or a road or a highway.

These corporations could make money as a repayment for their efforts. When a corporation operated a highway, for example, which could mean anything from providing a river crossing in a canoe to building slightly more sophisticated horse paths protected from trespassers by a fence, it earned income by charging tolls. Corporate profits were capped. Profits were permitted only to induce corporations to provide for the desired public good. Once a corporation completed the project for which it received its charter, the corporation was dissolved. Every charter was carefully considered before being granted; and few were.

Snapshot B: Personhood

Over time, corporations came to be viewed differently, and were granted ever greater latitude and power. Significantly, corporations were endowed with *personhood*, granting them many of the same rights as people. They could own property, enter into contracts, sue, or be sued. Of course, they couldn't marry or have children (but *do* they, in effect?), and they cannot vote. So how did corporations make the remarkable journey from being dissolved upon completing a single project to becoming "people"? It didn't happen all at once. As corporations gained power, they craved more — and fought for it in court. Eventually, corporate personhood — something never imagined in the constitution — arose from a combination of a legal clerk's sloppiness, lawyers' use of forged documents, and subsequent poor legal decision-making.[131] All the same, corporations' rights to act with naked self-interest were now established.

Thousands of connected dots later, corporations' right to freedom of speech under the First Amendment lets them spend unlimited amounts of money in influencing elections. And so they do, above and below the table, to further their interests.

Snapshot C: Off the rails

By the early 2000s, the lack of scrutiny into a company's reasons for incorporating would have shocked the country's founders, who were all too wary of overly powerful corporations. *The People's Business*[132] tells a humorous, true — but harrowing — story: For a fee of $130 and without a peep from Virginia's Secretary of State, a new company was born. Like all legal companies (in Virginia and elsewhere), it could grow as large as it liked, remain a company forever, and enjoy limited liability under law. And engage in whatever business practices it wanted, as long as they were legal. This particular company declared in its articles of incorporation:

> The purpose of the corporation is to engage in any business permitted by the Commonwealth of Virginia and not required to be stated herein including, but not limited to, the manufacture and marketing of tobacco products in a way that each year kills over 400,000 Americans and 4.5 million other persons worldwide.[133]

The new company's name: Licensed to Kill, Inc. It never intended to sell cigarettes, of course. It wanted to use its corporate status only to point out how morally bankrupt companies could be while remaining within the law. Its initial press release read:

> Licensed to Kill, Inc. is pretty much like any other tobacco company. We kill to make a profit. . . . We would like to especially thank the Commonwealth of Virginia's State Corporation Commission for granting us permission to exist. If a person was to ask the state for authorization to go on a serial killing rampage, he would surely be locked up in jail or a mental institution. Luckily, such moral standards do not apply to corporations.[134]

Only its rhetoric — not the actions it could take if it so chose — separates it from companies like Altria that do sell cigarettes. The same press release states, "The main difference [from actual tobacco companies] is that we're very upfront about our purpose."

Even with the link between smoking and illness or death having been unequivocally established, major tobacco companies continue to legally sell their products. These companies are not, of course, the only ones whose practices cause public harm. Energy companies continue to produce fossil fuels, far in advance of the Earth's capacity to withstand the consequences. Social media companies like Facebook operate in ways that compromise truth and allow democracy to be undermined. And the list goes on.

Snapshot D: A future

With the nation still poised for advances in civil rights in the wake of ongoing Black Lives Matter demonstrations of 2020, one of the great champions of the civil rights movement passed away.

John Lewis, a fiery student leader who became the "conscience of Congress," where he served for over 30 years, died on July 17, 2020. Days before his death, he wrote an op-ed which he asked the *New York Times* to publish on the day of his funeral. The *Times* published it with a title taken from one of its lines: "Together, you can redeem the soul of our nation."[135] Lewis wrote about his unwavering life's ambition to achieve civil rights. The speech is a masterpiece. It spells out a future that lies in front of us, if we do the necessary work:

> While my time here has now come to an end, I want you to know that in the last days and hours of my life you inspired me. You filled me with hope about the next chapter of the great American story when you used your power to make a difference in our society. Millions of people motivated simply by human compassion laid down the burdens of division. Around the country and the world you set aside race, class, age, language and nationality to demand respect for human dignity.

That is why I had to visit Black Lives Matter Plaza in Washington, though I was admitted to the hospital the following day. I just had to see and feel it for myself that, after many years of silent witness, the truth is still marching on.

. . .

[As a young person,] I heard the voice of Dr. Martin Luther King Jr. on an old radio. He was talking about the philosophy and discipline of nonviolence. He said we are all complicit when we tolerate injustice. He said it is not enough to say it will get better by and by. He said each of us has a moral obligation to stand up, speak up and speak out. When you see something that is not right, you must say something. You must do something. Democracy is not a state. It is an act, and each generation must do its part to help build what we called the Beloved Community, a nation and world society at peace with itself.

Ordinary people with extraordinary vision can redeem the soul of America by getting in what I call good trouble, necessary trouble.

. . . Continue to build union between movements stretching across the globe because we must put away our willingness to profit from the exploitation of others.

Though I may not be here with you, I urge you to answer the highest calling of your heart and stand up for what you truly believe. In my life I have done all I can to demonstrate that the way of peace, the way of love and nonviolence is the more excellent way. Now it is your turn to let freedom ring.

"Democracy is not a state. It is an act, and each generation must do its part." This assertion applies as much to the future as it does to democracy. The future's time is now.

Appendix 1

SHOPPING
APPS

These apps provide different lenses to help you shop in alignment with your values. As of fall 2022, all apps were available, easy to download, and worked like they were supposed to. We're talking about apps for mobile here (unless it says anything to the contrary); however, there are links to websites, if you need them, to help you find the apps or find out more about the company behind them.

Good On You — Ethical Fashion

➤ Find ethical clothing brands
📱 *App: link in the contextual menu*

Good On You synthesizes information from company reports, third-party evaluations, independent certifications, and more to rate brands on a five-point scale from "We Avoid" to "Great," based on their treatment of the planet, people, and animals.

Use it to check if your favorite brands are acting in ways you think are ethical and receive suggestions for sustainable brands to replace those that are not. It offers special deals on clothes from socially responsible brands, plus articles on sustainable fashion.

Too Good to Go

➤ Pick up about-to-be-discarded food at a 50% discount

📱 *App: link on homepage*

Too Good to Go is combatting food waste by connecting restaurants and stores, and the food they can no longer sell commercially, with willing local buyers at a discounted price. In addition, the app has an extensive "Knowledge Hub" about food waste.

The company launched in 2016 in Copenhagen, and has since spread quickly across Europe. Its current expansion into the United States is limited, but growing.

Goods Unite Us

➤ Link brands to politics

📱 *App*

Goods Unite Us shows which political organizations and campaigns companies are supporting. It does so in a clean, well-recognized, and easy-to-use interface.

Think Dirty
➤ Clean cosmetics

📱 *App: link on homepage*

This app focuses on selling safe, non-toxic, healthful (and *possibly* safer for the environment) beauty products. It covers 1.4 million products and allows barcode scanning. A well-put-together website.

ThredUp
➤ Sustainable brands

📱 *App (Android only)*

ThredUp is an online thrift (and consignment) store that leverages technology to support a hassle-free, affordable "circular" fashion economy, which benefits the climate and saves customers money. The mobile app and website allow you to buy or sell over 35,000 brands of clothes. Its website (only) helps you identify top sustainable brands, from everyday to sustainable "luxe."

Makeena
➤ Healthier foods and eco-friendly products

📱 *App: link on homepage*

Find responsible brands by name, category (apparel, beverages, etc.), or attribute (e.g., gluten-free or fair trade). Get money back on nearly all products. Makeena provides further financial incentive to shop greener and cleaner by partnering with hundreds of socially responsible brands to provide exclusive rewards on nearly all clean and green products. It's easy to use: scan an item's barcode and snap a picture of your receipt in the app. Makeena is a B Corp.

DoneGood

➤ Intentional spending to support people and the planet

DoneGood offers products from both U.S. and foreign companies that are more environmentally friendly and treat workers well. DoneGood has compiled a searchable database of clothes, accessories, coffee, tea, self-care products and more — all from small-scale sustainable brands. An easy-to-use platform on mobile.

Progressive Shopper

➤ Find companies with progressive values

🖥 *Browser extension*

This website (and Chrome browser extension) examines political contributions filed with the Federal Election Commission to help users find companies that align with progressive values. Users can see the campaign funding a company has given to the two main U.S. political parties' candidates and committees expressed as a percentage of Democratic versus Republican. It can also be used to rate companies on issues including: deforestation/fossil fuels; support for the gun industry; denial of the climate crisis; and other issues.

❖ ❖ ❖

Kiss the Ground, an organization devoted to regenerative agriculture, has a purchasing guide in line with these principles. Regenerative agriculture helps rebuild the planet, not just slow down its destruction. The guide covers the gamut of ways we can #EATFORTHECLIMATE.

The *Guardian* newspaper contains ethical purchasing guides for fashion, food and beverages, education, and lifestyle & beauty. Guides provide tips, list apps, and point you at social enterprises selling ethical products.

A research study by T.P.L. Nghiem and L.R. Carrasco[136] looked at 32 apps purporting to promote environmental sustainability, on land and in the oceans. It found many lacking in methodological rigor or transparency. A list of apps (many covering seafood or personal care) is downloadable as part of the paper's supplementary data.

Appendix 2

WATCHDOGS AND GUIDED PURCHASING

Organization	Focus areas	Features
Justmeans.com	Corporate social responsibility, sustainable development, health, energy, technology and innovation.	Online community. Content produced by professional journalists, distributed through mainstream news outlets.
Ethical Consumer	Ethical consumption: energy, food, technology, sustainability, and more.	Tools (free and with subscription) to guide ethical purchasing. Research-based ratings of companies and products. Lists: Best Buys, What Not to Buy.
RE100	Environmental behavior of large, electricity-consuming companies. Member companies publicly commit to 100% renewable energy by 2050.	Annual progress reports. Goal: accelerate adoption of zero-carbon electricity.

Organization	Focus areas	Features
DoneGood.co	Identifies and lists relatively unknown, affordable brands that are addressing issues including poverty alleviation and climate change.	Sells products and receives commissions. Goal: incubate companies that are "good for people" and "good for the planet," and to inspire larger companies to copy their business practices.
Human Rights Watch	Documents and fights human rights abuses in many forms: children, refugees and migrants, the environment, and much more.	Detailed reports across sectors and geographies. Documents both abuses and progress made.
Political Economy Research Institute (PERI)	Original research to promote human and ecological wellbeing. Translates findings into policy.	Publishes reports and working papers. Technical research.
International Labour Organization (ILO)	Labor standards, policy, and programs.	Reports, trends, statistics.
Amnesty International	Research and campaigning against human rights abuses. Advocacy and lobbying.	Human rights education and courses (including an app). Campaigns.
Environmental Working Group	Consumer choice for a healthier environment. Consumer goods, energy, food, and water.	Consumer guides and research. Lists, guides, and databases.

Appendix 3

HOW TO SUPPORT LOCAL BUSINESS

What are our options if we want to support local businesses?

We start by giving some thought to what we buy. Each purchase we make involves a decision — but very often that decision is an almost subconscious one to repeat our previous behavior. Pause a little and make a more conscious choice. One such decision hinges on local versus non-local. Where we decide to place our custom helps determine what stores stay open; which in turn determines which jobs are lost and which retained. Since local stores "hang together" in an ecosystem, by supporting one you are, in a sense, supporting many.

Avoid non-local

Amazon takes a big bite out of local businesses, forcing many to close or retrench. The answer to this is obvious: don't buy from Amazon. Yet Amazon has succeeded in making itself part of our culture, with its ease of use, enormous range of products, and low prices. Why don't we try to make choosing not to buy there more of a reflexive action? I buy from Amazon, but only as a last resort: When I can, I choose an alternative: my local bookstore, my local hardware store, my local bike shop. When I can't, then Amazon.

Similarly, when Wal-Mart begins looking around our neighborhood with a view to building a new store, what then? We can voice our concerns. As we've noted, a newly installed Wal-Mart can close down a lot of local stores — sporting goods stores, clothing stores, pet shops, etc. And the businesses with which those stores interact — local media, local lawyers, local suppliers, and others — may all be undone by the next wave of effects. So we can tell our local city council members to keep Wal-Mart away.

As for state or local government trying to lure large, out-of-state businesses to your hometown: tell them not to waste your money like that (see Box 1).

Buy local

To preserve our communities' character — and even their ability to provide quality public services — we can buy local. Yes, big-box stores may have "everyday low prices." Amazon's prices may be even lower. But buying online, just as buying from large, national chain stores, allows our purchasing and tax dollars to "leak" out of our communities. Favoring low prices over local commerce inevitably hollows out our communities. Low prices come at a cost.

Box 1

Local governments receive nearly half of their revenue from property taxes, not counting any money received from state or federal governments. School funding is especially dependent on this money. Which makes local governments' actions seem strange when they try to attract out-of-state businesses by letting them off the hook for their property taxes.

States and communities can act against their best interests when they try to attract new businesses, even new industries. Michigan, my home state, wanted to become a hub for film and TV. It offered a combination of tax credits and cash incentives to get movies made here, including *Batman vs. Superman* and the *Transformer* series, not to mention the blockbuster *The Godfather of Green Bay*. After two years, $500–650 million in state incentives generated less than two-thirds that much in private-sector spending. In other words, the state lost about a quarter billion dollars trying to out-Hollywood Hollywood (and Georgia). Michigan mercifully let its incentive program die.[137] New York similarly succumbed, spending as much on film tax credits as it could have spent for 5,000 additional public-school teachers.[138]

Do we want this?

"Local" can be however you define it. If you live in New York City or San Francisco, local probably needs to be scaled down to something smaller, like your neighborhood. Even if you live in a smaller town, you may identify with one part of it more than others. All the same, it is not hard to figure out which is the local option: Starbucks or Roos Roast; a Coors or a Massacre (15% alcohol, brewed by Wolverine State Brewery); Sam's Clothing Store or Target; Amazon or . . . well, almost anything.

If the price of buying local is a concern, be a 15%er. Begin by "buying local" one day a week; purchase *some* locally grown vegetables, not all your produce; get that next book from your local bookstore, even if you still get your exotic deodorant from Amazon. Some, not all. At least to start. When you get the hang of it, you can consider doing more.

Local restaurants

Local restaurants lend distinctiveness and personality to a community. Yet restaurants have been among the businesses hardest-hit by Covid. About 15% of them have closed their doors forever, laying off three million people. During the coronavirus, many of us supported them by ordering takeout — a habit that we might like to persist with if disinclined to dine out (but consider ordering direct; see below). Some restaurants let you buy gift cards — which essentially means you're making them a loan. (Others go even further, allowing you to invest in them, a topic covered in Chapter 9, "Investing for Real Impact.")

But it's not just pandemics that are damaging to our restaurants. If you use GrubHub, Uber Eats, or DoorDash, you accept higher prices — between 7% and 91% higher.[139] But what's convenient (and safe) for us isn't good for restaurants. In good times, restaurants operate on low profit margins, about the 5% mark. Costs for rent, food, and labor eat up about 90% of the money they take in. Apps then tack on an additional 20–30% of each order in fees the restaurant must pay.[140] During the height of the pandemic, apps accounted for almost 90% of sales at surviving restaurants, where sales have dropped 15% overall.[141] It's not hard to see why restaurants are struggling.

App makers squeeze restaurants. Their fees are non-negotiable. They create fake, virtual restaurants by combining competitors' menus. They now own the domain names of tens of thousands of local, independent restaurants, substituting their own phone numbers for those of the restaurants. You may not even realize you're supporting these apps when you order. Food delivery apps have become giant businesses. GrubHub, DoorDash, and Uber Eats are now stocks you can own (the latter as part of Uber Technologies), with total values of about $7 billion, $40 billion, and $92 billion, respectively. Investors think they will become *the* way for us to "take out" and dine at home. With so much money at their disposal, these app-delivery companies can afford to outwait any competition; as of now, they are not even profitable.

Local restaurants, meanwhile, must rely on their own resources to survive — they don't have deep-pocketed investors keeping them afloat in tough times. The drivers that are hired by the delivery apps: they are scraping by, too.[142]

Delivery apps represent yet another example of "gig aggregators." These companies use resources belonging to others — other people's cars, or homes, and now their restaurants — to offer us choice and convenience. But they dictate financial terms, and they are not satisfied with taking a small cut of each transaction; they simply rely on their massive scale to make a handsome profit. They favor not only a large slice of each transaction but an ever-increasing scale as well.

Just as Amazon reshaped the way we shop for so many of our goods, gig aggregators are shaping the way we eat (and get around, and find lodging away from home). If the "Amazon way" makes you uneasy, expect the same in these new industries, restaurants included. And apps are winning the battle for mindshare, convincing an overwhelming majority of California's voters not to reclassify gig workers as employees (who would then be entitled to retirement benefits, health insurance, and other benefits) but rather to keep them designated as contractors. GrubHub, along with Uber and Lyft, spent nearly $200 million in engineering this outcome.[143]

What can we do?

We can go to real, physical, local restaurants — when it's safe to do so, depending on the coronavirus situation, which was entering an unrestricted phase as this was being written. And when you want to eat pizza or any other takeout at home, order directly from the restaurants themselves. If they don't have their own drivers (check), go pick up the food yourself.

There might be some glimmers of hope where food delivery is concerned. In Washington, D.C., for example, an upstart food delivery service is trying to make things better for restaurants (through lower fees), couriers (offering better jobs, including fixed hours at better wages), and customers (whose delivery times are honored).[144] For now, this is just a glaring exception to the rule.

Local food

The most nutritious food we can eat is the freshest, most recently harvested. It is that which is transported short distances (requiring little fossil fuel) and it often uses less harmful packaging.

In short, it is local.

The farming methods that are doing the very best to protect us against the ravages of climate change are *regenerative* ones. The farms on which such methods are used are often local, too. Regenerative agriculture surpasses the less ambitious notion of "sustainable agriculture," which implies staying within known system limits. Regenerative agriculture, in contrast, can actually improve the health of the planet. A key feature is rebuilding the soil. Regenerative practices capture carbon in plants' cells and in the soil in which they grow. In turn, the soil is vibrantly alive with microorganisms, supporting healthier life above and below ground. Even if we stopped emitting carbon today, we are still in trouble because there is far too much in the atmosphere right now, already causing great harm. Regenerative farming can reduce this accumulation of CO_2,[145] a benefit accruing on top of its replacement of conventional agriculture with its harmful practices, including razing trees and forests to grow crops, using dangerous synthetic chemicals, and destroying the soil's integrity — all of which imperil our land, water, skies, and future.

Supporting regenerative agriculture is important, and supporting local food systems is an effective way to do that. But only some locally grown food is produced this way. You have to ask the farmers at your farmers' market, or your CSA (community supported agriculture; i.e., farms that sell you "shares" of what they grow). Ask questions like these: How do you keep the soil fertile? Do you rotate crops? A much fuller explanation of regenerative agriculture, including many more questions you could ask, can be found in Kiss the Ground's useful report.[146]

Local farms compete against larger, better-funded industrial farms, which are very unlikely to be at the forefront of regeneration, sustainability, or anything else other than maximizing productivity and profit. By supporting healthful, local farms, we encourage their success, which in turn spreads the knowledge and application of their methods.

When you can't find acceptable local produce, check out traditional companies and brands — they are not all the same. USDA Organic, Demeter Biodynamic, and other certifications can also let you know what to put on your plate that is good for both you and the planet.

Appendix 4

TOOLS FOR FINDING EFFECTIVE CHARITIES

To guide our giving, we can look to "meta-charities," which examine other charities' effectiveness. Some are listed here, along with other resources.

GiveWell searches for charities that perform best at saving or improving lives (per dollar donated). They use rigorous research to support their recommendations.

Giving Green uses an evidence-based approach to support people's donations of money or time to combat the climate crisis.

Animal Charity Evaluators analyzes and supports rigorous research to help us understand the most effective ways to help animals. Sixty billion animals are raised and killed each year for food. Animal Charity Evaluators places its concern on the suffering of both these and animals in the wild.

The Life You Can Save Founded by Peter Singer, this organization translates his seminal work on "effective altruism" into tools and advice that support our charitable giving.

❖ ❖ ❖

An article on Vox.com[147] serves as a primer on giving effectively. It contains 10 guidelines to help us give with more impact.

Another article on Vox.com[148] recommends seven high-impact, evidence-based organizations fighting the climate crisis.

Appendix 5

TOOLS FOR FINDING GOOD BANKS AND CREDIT UNIONS

As we saw in Chapter 7, not all banks are the same. It matters where we bank. But evaluating such choices can seem daunting. Here is a list of resources to help you do just that.

Mighty is a bank comparison site. It analyzes public data from all banks and credit unions that report on how they invest customers' money. It encourages banks to increase their sustainability transparency. **This is a direct link** to its "Find banks" tool.

The **Institute for Local Self-Reliance** provides information and a tool to find local banks and credit unions. **This is a direct link** to its "find banks" tool.

The **Community Development Financial Institution Fund** (U.S. Department of Treasury) lists CDFIs, by state. **This is a direct link** to its "certification" page.

BankLocal rates banks and credit unions in the vicinity of a user's hometown.

BankImpact, part of **National Community Investment Fund**, searches and compares banks.

The **US SIF** (Forum for Sustainable and Responsible Investment) links to community development banks and credit unions. **This is a direct link** to its "accreditation" page.

Certified B Corporations. To access the directory, **go here**, where you can see the full list of B-Corps.

◈ ◈ ◈

An article on NerdWallet[149] also serves as a tool to find Black banks.

Appendix 6

TOOLS FOR RESPONSIBLE AND SUSTAINABLE INVESTING

In Chapter 9 we looked at investing and how to identify investments with positive societal impact. Here are the links to the tools mentioned in that chapter, plus a few others.

The **Global Reporting Initiative (GRI) Sustainability Disclosure Database** is a search tool for sustainability reports. It can be accessed by signing up to **corporateregister.com** (which is free).

Principles for Responsible Investment (or PRI principles): an ESG framework which subscribing financial institutions commit to follow. Overview (as a PDF document) **available here**. Questions to ask prospective financial advisors can be found in *A Practical Guide to ESG Integration for Equity Investing* (**PDF document**).

Morningstar Sustainability Ratings/ESG screener.

The **U.S. Department of Labor** reviews over two dozen ESG investment tools. PDF document **available here.**

An article on **CrowdWise**[150] on the leading investment crowdfunding websites.

Investibule has a **slideshow** on "Community Capital 2000" (investing in local businesses) which contains a chart showing numerous local investment crowdfunding platforms. Out of those 31, the following 25 are still in operation at time of going to press: WeFunder; StartEngine; SeedInvest; Kiva; Republic; Netcapital; NextSeed; MicroVentures; Credibles; Honeycomb Credit; Mainvest; GrowthFountain; Crowdfund Mainstreet; Mr. Crowd; Small Change; Wunderfund; Milk Money; truCrowd; Gridshare; Rabble; SVXUS; FlashFunders; Venture; Jumpstart Micro; In Kind Direct.[151]

The **National Coalition for Community Capital** lists examples of community investment funds in **this PDF document** subtitled "A How-To Guide for Building Local Wealth, Equity, and Justice".

ImpactAlpha is an online publication which describes many areas of impact investing, including opportunities open for investment.

Appendix 7

CARBON OFFSET TOOLS

The tools below help you calculate your carbon footprint or buy carbon offsets to compensate for the carbon you're responsible for. Some do both. Note if you "pay" for an offset with a donation (or support an organization registered as a U.S. charity), you may get a tax deduction. When you purchase an offset, you do not.

Carbon Footprint, Ltd has a footprint calculator and offers projects matching the amount of carbon you choose to offset.

Carbonfund.org accepts donations to purchase carbon offsets: annual offsets (for individuals, families, or businesses); car use; travel; and other options. The offsets cover a variety of projects.

Carbon Offsets to Alleviate Poverty has useful information about reducing your carbon. It has a footprint calculator and lets you buy offsets. Reforestation and similar projects are developed in low-income countries and provide jobs. It crowdsources funding (from individuals) to pay for the offsets, to provide tree planters/farm workers with income, and to provide food from orchards.

Clear is a B Corp that calculates and offsets personal carbon. It is distinguished by careful vetting of projects and accurate calculators.

Climate Trust is a non-profit that develops U.S.-based projects. It sells carbon offsets to voluntary and compliance purchasers.

Cool Effect is a non-profit organization focused on identifying and offering offsets with a high degree of certainty of reducing emissions.

myclimate calculates and offsets your carbon.

Native Energy calculates your carbon footprint and purchases offsets.

Sustainable Travel International promotes more sustainable travel through awareness, carbon measurement, carbon reduction projects, carbon offsets, and protection of threatened ecosystems.

Terrapass offers subscriptions so individuals can regularly offset their carbon, plus *à la carte* offerings used in counteracting the carbon associated with travel or special events like weddings, and even as gifts. It also allows the purchase of carbon credits (from compliance markets) to retire them.

Wren, a subscription site, aims to make individuals — its "members" — feel more empowered by guiding them towards projects that they can contribute to, such as tree planting, conservation, technology R&D, and policy work.

❖ ❖ ❖

If you want to dig a bit deeper, look for projects that are verified, enforceable, permanent, and additional. This last term means that, without this organization's activities, the desired result would not have occurred (i.e., no one would have done it). Similarly, avoid projects where there is "leakage" — meaning carbon-producing behavior simply moves from one location to another.

You may be able to buy offsets for air travel through an airline. But they do not make it easy; and you, not they, will be paying, even though they might be claiming credit and garnering the rewards in the shape of good PR or tax breaks.

Not listed in this appendix are organizations whose job it is to verify and certify the amount of carbon avoided or reduced or to set the standards followed in this process. Both play an important role in enabling us to trust that we are buying something that genuinely helps the planet; but we generally don't interact with them as individuals.

Endnotes

Introduction

1 Terry Nguyen and Christina Animashaun, "How the coronavirus is disrupting us air travel, in 2 charts." *Vox*, April 20, 2020. https://www.vox.com/the-goods/2020/4/20/21224080/coronavirus-air-travel-decline-charts.

Chapter 1: Give It Your 15%

2 David Wallace-Wells, *The Uninhabitable Earth: Life after Warming* (New York: Tim Duggan Books, 2019).

3 Intergovernmental Panel on Climate Change (IPCC), *Climate Change 2022: Impacts, Adaptation and Vulnerability. Summary for Policymakers* (2022). https://www.ipcc.ch/report/ar6/wg2/downloads/report/IPCC_AR6_WGII_SummaryForPolicymakers.pdf.

Chapter 2: Be Reciprocal

4 Dan Ariely, "Americans want to live in a much more equal country (they just don't realize it)." *The Atlantic*, August 2, 2012. https://www.theatlantic.com/business/archive/2012/08/

americans-want-to-live-in-a-much-more-equal-country-they-just-dont-realize-it/260639.

5 Judy Wicks, "Good morning, beautiful business." Twenty-fourth Annual E.F. Schumacher Lecture, October 2004. https://centerforneweconomics.org/publications/good-morning-beautiful-business.

Chapter 3: Spend into the Future

6 Ian Livingston, "A giant heat dome over Alaska is set to threaten all-time temperature records." *Washington Post*, July 3, 2019. https://www.washingtonpost.com/weather/2019/07/03/giant-heat-dome-over-alaska-is-set-threaten-all-time-temperature-records.

7 Shekhar Chandra, "Are parts of India becoming too hot for humans?" CNN, July 4, 2019. https://www.cnn.com/2019/07/03/asia/india-heat-wave-survival-hnk-intl/index.html.

8 David Wallace-Wells, *op. cit.*

9 Everytown, "Gun violence in America." January 26, 2020. https://everytownresearch.org/report/gun-violence-in-america.

10 Daniel M. Zane, Julie R. Irwin, and Rebecca Walker Reczek, "Do less ethical consumers denigrate more ethical consumers? The effect of willful ignorance of judgments of others." *Journal of Consumer Psychology* 26(3) (2016): 337–49. https://doi.org/10.1016/j.jcps.2015.10.002.

11 Edward M. Tauber, "Why do people shop?" *Journal of Marketing* 36(4) (1972): 46–49. https://www.jstor.org/stable/1250426.

12 J. Courtney Sullivan, "How diamonds became forever." *New York Times*, May 3, 2013. https://www.nytimes.com/2013/05/05/fashion/weddings/how-americans-learned-to-love-diamonds.html.

13 Edward Jay Epstein, "Have you ever tried to sell a diamond?" *The Atlantic*, February 1982. https://www.theatlantic.com/magazine/archive/1982/02/have-you-ever-tried-to-sell-a-diamond/304575.

14 GIA, "The origin of wedding rings: Ancient tradition or marketing invention?" https://4cs.gia.edu/en-us/blog/origin-of-wedding-rings.

15 Uri Friedman, "How an ad campaign invented the diamond engagement ring." *The Atlantic*, February 13, 2015. https://www.theatlantic.com/international/archive/2015/02/how-an-ad-campaign-invented-the-diamond-engagement-ring/385376

16 See https://en.wikipedia.org/wiki/GoodGuide.

17 Amazon Watch, "Complicity in destruction: How Northern consumers and financiers sustain the assault of the Brazilian Amazon and its peoples." September 11, 2018. https://amazonwatch.org/news/2018/0911-complicity-in-destruction.

Amazon Watch, "Complicity in destruction II: How Northern consumers and financiers enable Bolsanaro's assault on the Brazilian Amazon." April 25, 2019. https://amazonwatch.org/news/2019/0425-complicity-in-destruction-2.

Amazon Watch, "Complicity in destruction III: How global corporations enable violations of indigenous peoples' rights in the Brazilian Amazon." October 2020. https://amazonwatch.org/news/2020/1027-complicity-in-destruction-iii.

18 B Lab Global, "The B Impact Assessment." https://www.bcorporation.net/en-us/programs-and-tools/b-impact-assessment.

19 B Lab Global, "Find a B Corp." https://www.bcorporation.net/en-us/find-a-b-corp.

20 Mahlokoane Percy Ngwato, "Nielsen: Responsible brands are big business." *Business Chief*, May 19, 2020. https://www.businesschief.eu/digital-strategy/nielsen-responsible-brands-are-big-business-1.

21 Institute of Public & Environmental Affairs (IPE), "Welcome to the Institute of Public & Environmental Affairs." http://wwwen.ipe.org.cn/index.html.

22 Institute of Public & Environmental Affairs (IPE), "The Green Supply Chain Corporate Information Transparency Index." http://wwwen.ipe.org.cn/GreenSupplyChain/CITI.aspx.

23 Brian Stauffer, "Follow the thread: The need for supply chain transparency in the garment and footwear industry." Human Rights Watch, April 20, 2017. https://www.hrw.org/report/2017/04/20/follow-thread/need-supply-chain-transparency-garment-and-footwear-industry.

Chapter 4: Stay Home

24 Oxfam International, "World's billionaires have more wealth than 4.6 billion people." Press release, January 20, 2020. https://www.oxfam.org/en/press-releases/worlds-billionaires-have-more-wealth-46-billion-people.

25 Pew Research Center, "Trends in income and wealth inequality." January 9, 2020. https://www.pewresearch.org/social-trends/2020/01/09/trends-in-income-and-wealth-inequality.

26 Public Affairs Council, "Attitudes about big business and small business." 2015 Public Affairs Pulse Survey. https://pac.org/pulse/2015/attitudes-about-big-business-and-small-business.

27 Frank Newport, "Business gets bigger even as Americans prefer small." Gallup, August 22, 2017. https://news.gallup.com/opinion/

polling-matters/216674/business-gets-bigger-even-americans-prefer-small.aspx.

28 Congressional Research Service, *Small Business Administration and Job Creation*. January 4, 2018. https://sgp.fas.org/crs/misc/R41523.pdf.

29 Edward L. Glaeser and William R. Kerr, "The secret to job growth: Think small." *Harvard Business Review*, July–August 2010. https://hbr.org/2010/07/the-secret-to-job-growth-think-small.

30 Anil Rupasingha, *Locally Owned: Do Local Business Ownership and Size Matter for Local Economic Well-Being?* Federal Reserve Bank of Atlanta's Community and Economic Development Discussion Paper Series, 2013. https://www.atlantafed.org/-/media/documents/community-development/publications/discussion-papers/2013/01-do-local-business-ownership-size-matter-for-local-economic-well-being-2013-08-19.pdf.

31 Stephan Goetz and Anil Rupasingha, "Wal-Mart and social capital." *American Journal of Agricultural Economics* 88(5) (2006): 1,304–10. https://www.jstor.org/stable/4123608.

32 American Independent Business Institute, "The local multiplier effect: How independent local businesses help your community thrive." 2020. https://reclaimdemocracy.org/topics/independent-business.

33 Daniel J. Clark, "The 1950s were not a golden age for Detroit's autoworkers." What It Means to Be American, May 9, 2019. https://www.whatitmeanstobeamerican.org/places/the-1950s-were-not-a-golden-age-for-detroits-autoworkers.

34 Troy C. Blanchard, Charles Tolbert, and Carson Mencken, "The health and wealth of US counties: How the small business environment impacts alternative measures of development." *Cambridge Journal of Regions, Economy and Society* 5(1) (2012): 149–62. https://doi.org/10.1093/cjres/rsr034.

35 American Independent Business Alliance, "The multiplier effect of local independent businesses." https://www.amiba.net/resources/multiplier-effect.

36 Michael H. Shuman, *The Small-Mart Revolution: How Local Businesses Are Beating the Global Competition* (Oakland, CA: Berrett-Koehler Publishers, 2006).

37 Blanchard, Tolbert, and Mencken, *op. cit.*

38 David Graeber, *Debt: The First 5,000 Years* (Brooklyn, NY: Melville House, 2011).

39 Shankar Vedantam, "Emotional currency: How money shapes human relationships." NPR: Hidden Brain. January 13, 2020. https://www.npr.org/2020/01/10/795246685/emotional-currency-how-money-shapes-human-relationships?t=1657113519192.

40 Wicks, *op. cit.*

41 Graeber, *op. cit.*

42 "BerkShares: Our currency for the Berkshire region." https://www.berkshares.org.

Chapter 5: A Memo from Robert Frost

43 Raluca Dragusanu, E. Montero, and Nathan Nunn, "The effects of fair trade certification: Evidence from coffee producers in Costa Rica." Harvard University Department of Economics, forthcoming. https://scholar.harvard.edu/nunn/publications/impacts-fair-trade-certification-evidence-coffee-producers-costa-rica.

44 RMB Group, "Is coffee the last 'cheap' commodity?" May 24, 2018. https://www.rmbgroup.com/is-coffee-the-last-cheap-commodity.

45 Andrea Olivar "Without action, the future of coffee is not secure." *Daily Coffee News*, July 17, 2018. https://dailycoffeenews.com/2018/07/17/opinion-without-action-the-future-of-coffee-is-not-secure.

46 See, for example, "Fair pay towards a living income." Fair Trade Certified, July 12, 2022. https://www.fairtradecertified.org/blog/fair-pay-towards-a-living-income. "Fairtrade takes big step towards living wages for banana workers." Fairtrade International, December 15, 2020. https://www.fairtrade.net/news/fairtrade-big-step-living-wages-bananas.

Chapter 6: Two-Pocket Philanthropy

47 David W. Hutton, Hong-Gam Le, Srinivasan Aravind, Ravilla D. Ravindran, Haripriya Aravind, Thulasiraj Ravilla, Rengaraj Venkatesh, Alan L. Robin, and Joshua D. Stein, "The cost of cataract surgery at the Aravind Eye Hospital, India." *Investigative Opthamology & Visual Science* 55(13) (2014): 1,289. https://iovs.arvojournals.org/article.aspx?articleid=2266507.

48 Peter Singer, "Good charity, bad charity." *New York Times*, August 10, 2013. https://www.nytimes.com/2013/08/11/opinion/sunday/good-charity-bad-charity.html.

49 Also assuming that your sight is no more valuable or important than anyone else's.

50 Giving USA Foundation, *Giving USA 2020: The Annual Report of Philanthropy for the Year 2019*. https://store.givingusa.org/products/giving-usa-2020-the-annual-report-on-philanthropy-for-the-year-2019.

51 GiveWell, "Your dollar goes further overseas." https://www.givewell.org/giving101/Your-dollar-goes-further-overseas.

52 Dan Pallotta, "The way we think about charity is dead wrong." TED
   video, TED2013. https://www.ted.com/talks/dan_pallotta_the_way_we_
   think_about_charity_is_dead_wrong?language=en.
53 Charitable giving makes us feel good in ourselves. There is a vast
   literature on the relationship between income and happiness. Happiness
   itself can mean two very different things — how we feel moment-to-
   moment and how satisfied we are with our life as a whole. A pair of
   Nobel Prize winners, one an economist the other a psychologist, showed
   that the moment-to-moment kind of happiness won't increase after we
   reach an income of $75,000 (Daniel Kahneman and Angus Deaton, "High
   income improves evaluation of life but not emotional well-being." *PNAS*
   107[38] [August 4, 2010]: 16,489–93. https://www.pnas.org/doi/10.1073/
   pnas.1011492107). Life satisfaction (the other kind) will increase beyond
   that, but it takes a doubling of your income to boost your life satisfaction
   an extra unit. Saving money to spend on ourselves is a far from ideal
   way to become happier. Another stream of research looks at how we feel
   when we give to others (money and in other ways) (Jill Suttie and Jason
   Marsh, "5 ways giving is good for you." *Greater Good Magazine*, December
   13, 2010. https://greatergood.berkeley.edu/article/item/5_ways_giving_is_
   good_for_you). It shows several ways that giving is good for us: it makes
   us feel happier; it improves our health; it makes us feel closer to others;
   it makes us more grateful, a key to being happy. And our generosity
   inspires others to act generously, too. Peter Singer's arguments for
   effective altruism align with utilitarianism. From that perspective, we
   should do what promotes the greatest good or the greatest happiness.
   Yet Singer reminds us that giving makes us happy, too: "[T]hinking about
   the world as a whole, and identifying with a humanitarian tradition that
   has tried to make the world a better place can make *us* happier [emphasis
   mine]. . . . [B]eing part of a community that lives this way also helps"
   (Ezra Klein, "Peter Singer on the lives you can save." *Vox*, December
   6, 2019. https://www.vox.com/future-perfect/2019/12/6/20992100/
   peter-singer-effective-altruism-lives-you-can-save-animal-liberation).

Chapter 7: Don't Bank On It

54 Institute for Local Self-Reliance, "Share of deposits by size
   of institution, 1994 to 2018." May 14, 2019. https://ilsr.org/
   distribution-of-deposits-by-size-of-financial-institution.
55 Rachel Louise Ensign, "Biggest three banks gobble up
   $2.5 trillion in new deposits since crisis." *Wall Street
   Journal*, March 22, 2018. https://www.wsj.com/articles/

biggest-three-banks-gobble-up-2-4-trillion-in-new-deposits-since-crisis-1521711001.

56 Renae Merle, "A guide to the financial crisis — 10 years later." *Washington Post*, September 10, 2018. https://www.washingtonpost.com/business/economy/a-guide-to-the-financial-crisis--10-years-later/2018/09/10/114b76ba-af10-11e8-a20b-5f4f84429666_story.html?utm_term=.1123b41bf262.

57 Stacy Mitchell, "Understanding the small business credit crunch." Institute for Local Self-Reliance, April 16, 2014. https://ilsr.org/understanding-small-business-credit-crunch.

58 Stacy Mitchell, "One in four local banks has vanished since 2008: Here's what's causing the decline and why we should treat it as a national crisis." Institute for Local Self-Reliance, May 5, 2015. https://ilsr.org/vanishing-community-banks-national-crisis.

59 Olivia Lavecchia, "Percentage of bad loans by size of bank, 1999 to 2014." Institute for Local Self-Reliance, April 20, 2015. https://ilsr.org/percentage-of-bad-loans-by-size-of-bank.

60 Olivia Lavecchia, "Small business lending by size of institution, 2018." Institute for Local Self-Reliance, May 14, 2015. https://ilsr.org/small-business-lending-by-size-of-institution-2014.

61 Federal Reserve Bank of Cleveland and Federal Reserve Bank of Atlanta, *Small Business Credit Survey: Report on Minority-Owned Firms*. 2016. https://www.clevelandfed.org/~/media/content/community%20development/smallbusiness/2016%20sbcs/sbcs%20minority%20owned%20report.pdf?la=en.

62 Alexandra Killewald and Briella Bryan, "Does your home make you wealthy?" *RSF: The Russell Sage Foundation Journal of the Social Sciences* 2(6) (2016): 110–28. https://www.jstor.org/stable/10.7758/rsf.2016.2.6.06.

63 Thomas Boehm and Alan Schlottmann, *Wealth Accumulation and Homeownership: Evidence for Low-Income Households* (U.S. Department of Housing and Urban Development and Office of Policy Development & Research, 2004). https://www.huduser.gov/publications/pdf/wealthaccumulationandhomeownership.pdf.

64 Michael Neal, "Housing remains a key component of household wealth." HousingEconomics.com (National Association of Home Builders), September 3, 2013. http://www.nahbclassic.org/generic.aspx?genericContentID=215073&channelID=311.

65 *Ibid.*

66 Shuman, *op. cit.*

67 *Ibid.*

68 Martin Luther King Jr., "Martin Luther King, Jr. I've Been to the Mountaintop." American Rhetoric Top 100 Speeches. https://www.americanrhetoric.com/speeches/mlkivebeentothemountaintop.htm.

69 *Ibid.*

70 National Credit Union Administration, "NCUA releases Q1 2018 credit union system performance data." Press release, June 6, 2018. https://www.ncua.gov/newsroom/news/2018/ncua-releases-q1-2018-credit-union-system-performance-data.

71 BusinessWire, "Aspiration named a B Corp 2018 best for the world overall company." June 12, 2018. https://www.businesswire.com/news/home/20180612006269/en/Aspiration-Named-a-B-Corp-2018-Best-for-The-World-Overall-Company.

72 Eillie Anziilotti, "Are your buying habits remotely ethical? This bank account will tell you." *Fast Company*, April 26, 2017. https://www.fastcompany.com/40412509/are-your-buying-habits-remotely-ethical-this-bank-account-will-tell-you.

73 National Conference of State Legislatures, "The Upward Looking." 2010. http://www.ncsl.org/documents/sfn/UpwardLooking.pdf.

74 Until the Fair Housing Act of 1968, real estate agents could legally refuse to show Black people and other minorities homes in White neighborhoods, and banks could deny mortgages to such potential homebuyers even if they were shown the homes. For the next decade, poor people and People of Color were also denied other types of credit, based on perceived risk. In 1977, the Community Reinvestment Act was enacted to correct this financial discrimination by making banks support the credit needs of the low- and moderate-income communities in which they were licensed to operate. By law, banks' records in meeting these needs are now periodically evaluated. Banks that fail to meet their obligations to serve communities' credit needs can be denied banking privileges.

75 Oscar Gonzales, "Snap Stat: Sizing up CDFIs." CDFI Fund, June 1, 2016. https://www.cdfifund.gov/impact/17.

76 National Community Investment Fund and Initiative for Responsible Investment, *Doing Business with Community Development Banking Institutions: A Deposits Initiative.* 2010. http://iri.hks.harvard.edu/files/iri/files/doing_business_with_community_development_banking_institutions_a_deposits_initiative.pdf.

77 Calvert Impact Capital, Inc., "Community Investment Note: Everyone can invest in solutions to inequality and climate change." 2018. https://calvertimpactcapital.org/investing/community-investment-note.

78 Calvert Impact Capital, "Community Investment Note: Everyone can invest in solutions to inequality and climate change." 2018. https://calvertimpactcapital.org/investing/community-investment-note [scroll down to "Frequently Asked Questions."]

Chapter 8: Cut Them Up

79 Robert Muggah, Adriaana Abdeneur, and Ilona Szabó, "Fighting climate change means fighting organized crime." *Project Syndicate*, March 12, 2019. https://www.project-syndicate.org/commentary/amazon-illegal-mining-climate-change-by-robert-muggah-et-al-2019-03.

80 Eliane Brum, "The death of the last Juma elder in the Amazon." *New York Times*, April 2, 2021. https://www.nytimes.com/2021/04/02/opinion/international-world/juma-people-brazil-amazon.html.

81 Ward Warmerdam, *European and North American Supply Chain and Financial Relationships Linked to Brazilian Environmental Offenders*. Profundo, April 9, 2019. https://www.profundo.nl/download/aw1904-financial-links.

82 FAIRR, "Deforestation in the Cerrado." FAIRR: A Coller Initiative, May 14, 2019. https://www.fairr.org/article/cerrado-deforestation.

83 Wallace-Wells, *op. cit.*

84 Shannon Hall, "Exxon knew about climate change almost 40 years ago." *Scientific American*, October 26, 2015. https://www.scientificamerican.com/article/exxon-knew-about-climate-change-almost-40-years-ago.

85 Jane Mayer, *Dark Money: The Hidden History of the Billionaires behind the Rise of the Radical Right* (New York: Anchor Books, 2016).

86 350.Org, "350.Org on JP Morgan Chase's new climate announcement." Press release, February 25, 2020. https://350.org/press-release/chase-climate-announcement.

87 Rainforest Action Network, Banktrack, Indigenous Environmental Network, OilChange, Reclaim Finance, and Sierra Club, *Banking on Climate Chaos: Fossil Fuel Finance Report, 2021*. https://www.ran.org/wp-content/uploads/2021/03/Banking-on-Climate-Chaos-2021.pdf.

88 *Ibid.*

89 Amazon Watch, "Complicity in destruction II . . ." (2019).

90 Bill McKibben, "Money is the oxygen on which the fire of global warming burns." *The New Yorker*, September 17, 2018. https://www.newyorker.com/news/daily-comment/money-is-the-oxygen-on-which-the-fire-of-global-warming-burns.

91 Taylor Tepper, "The credit card reward game is unfair? But is it unethical?" *New York Times*, March 11, 2019.

92 Credit.com, "The weirdest cards you can get." May 27, 2018. https://www.credit.com/blog/the-weirdest-credit-cards-you-can-get-83066.

93 The B Impact Assessment itself leaves some wiggle room in this regard. In its theory of change, it states, ". . . any company that is committed to creating social and environmental impact, whatever their previous activities, can consider certification" and even suggests an oil company might qualify if it were beginning to replace fossil fuels with renewable energy sources. So a bit of scrutiny about a bank's lending may provide a bit more reassurance (https://www.aspiration.com/spendandsave).

94 https://www.aspiration.com/spendandsave.

Chapter 9: Investing for Real Impact

95 Madison Sargis and Patrick Wang, "How does investing in ESG companies affect returns?" Morningstar, February 19, 2020. https://www.morningstar.com/insights/2020/02/19/esg-companies. Matthew Heimer, "Why a data revolution is giving socially responsible investors an edge." *Fortune*, September 25, 2019. https://fortune.com/2019/09/25/esg-investing-stocks-data-revolution.

96 UNEP Finance Initiative and United Nations Global Compact, *Principles for Responsible Investment*. 2021. https://www.unpri.org/download?ac=10948.

97 U.S. Securities & Exchange Commission, "JPMorgan Chase Shareholder Proposal," 2020. See Interfaith Center on Corporate Responsibility (ICCR), "JPMorgan aims to silence shareholder seeking reporting on fossil fuel financing." February 12, 2020. https://www.iccr.org/jpmorgan-aims-silence-shareholder-seeking-reporting-fossil-fuel-financing.

98 Carolyn Price, "1000% growth in online private market investors." Kingscrowd, October 20, 2021. https://kingscrowd.com/1000-percent-growth-online-private-market-investors.

99 Jonny Price, "Rule change could spur $1 billion in crowdfunded investment." ImpactAlpha, March 15, 2021. https://impactalpha.com/rule-changes-could-spur-1-billion-in-crowdfunded-investment.

100 See "90 Best Crowdfunding Blogs and Websites" at https://blog.feedspot.com/crowdfunding_blogs.

101 Brian Beckon, Amy Cortese, Jeff Rosen, Janice Shade, and Michael H. Shuman, *Community Investment Funds: A How-to Guide for Building Local Wealth, Equity, and Justice* (National Coalition for Community Capital and The Solidago Foundation, 2021). https://bdgiving.org.uk/wp-content/uploads/2021/04/Community-Investment-Funds-Final.pdf.

102 Michael Gordon, *Becoming a Social Entrepreneur: Starting Out, Scaling Up, Staying True* (Abingdon, UK: Routledge, 2019). https://profmichaelgordon.com/books/becoming-a-social-entrepreneur.

103 John Bloom, "RSF rate changes: Interest beyond the price." RSF Social Finance, April 2, 2020. https://rsfsocialfinance.org/2020/04/02/rsf-rate-changes-interest-beyond-the-price.

104 KarmaTube, "The power of the mindful minute at work." Video. https://www.karmatube.org/videos.php?id=7515.

Chapter 10: Don't Eat Breakfast

105 Jonathan Franzen, "What if we stopped pretending?" *The New Yorker*, September 8, 2019. https://www.newyorker.com/culture/cultural-comment/what-if-we-stopped-pretending.

106 "Table of solutions." Project Drawdown. https://drawdown.org/solutions/table-of-solutions.

107 Rare and California Environmental Associates (CEA), *Changing Behaviors to Reduce U.S. Emissions: Seven Pathways to Achieve Climate Impact* (Arlington, VA: Rare, 2019). https://behavior.rare.org/wp-content/uploads/2020/09/Changing-behaviors-to-reduce-U.S.-emissions-20200902.pdf.

108 Union of Concerned Scientists, *Going from Pump to Plug: Adding up the Savings from Electric Vehicles*. 2017. https://www.ucsusa.org/sites/default/files/attach/2017/11/cv-report-ev-savings.pdf.

109 Kelley Hamrick and Melissa Gallant, *Unlocking Potential: State of the Voluntary Carbon Markets 2017* (Washington, D.C.: Forest Trends Ecosystem Marketplace, 2017). https://www.forest-trends.org/publications/unlocking-potential

110 ImpactAlpha, "Rising price of carbon starts to hit balance sheets — and corporate decision-making." February 3, 2022. https://impactalpha.com/rising-price-of-carbon-starts-to-hit-balance-sheets-and-corporate-decision-making.

111 Nina Chestney, "Global carbon markets value surged to record $851 bln last year — Refinitiv." Reuters, January 31, 2022. https://www.reuters.com/business/energy/global-carbon-markets-value-surged-record-851-bln-last-year-refinitiv-2022-01-31.

112 ImpactAlpha, *op. cit.*

113 Hamrick and Gallant, *op. cit.*

114 It is also possible to buy carbon credits on mandatory markets and then "retire" them. Once they have been taken out of circulation, no company can buy them to balance out its emissions.

115 Jennifer Cooper. "How carbon offset projects can improve health and wellbeing." Native: A Public Benefit Corporation, December 20, 2017. https://native.eco/2017/12/how-carbon-offset-projects-can-improve-health-and-wellbeing.

116 Rare and California Environmental Associates, *op. cit.*

117 Bill McKibben, "Renewable energy is suddenly startlingly cheap." *The New Yorker*, April 28, 2021.

118 Rupert Way, Matthew C. Ives, Penny Mealy, and Doyne Farme, "Empirically grounded technology forecasts and the energy transition." *Joule* 6(9): 2,057–82. https://www.cell.com/joule/fulltext/S2542-4351(22)00410-X.

119 Bill McKibben, "Betting on gas in definitely immoral — and probably unwise." *The New Yorker*, July 16, 2020. https://www.newyorker.com/news/annals-of-a-warming-planet/betting-on-gas-is-definitely-immoral-and-probably-unwise.

120 Bill McKibben, "We're finally catching a break in the climate fight." The Crucial Years, September 19, 2021. https://billmckibben.substack.com/p/were-finally-catching-a-break-in.

121 She won the first-ever Gulbenkian Prize for Humanity for her work on protecting the planet. She then promptly gave away the entire €1 million prize to front-line organizations combatting the climate crisis.

122 "Face the Climate Emergency." Climate Emergency Europe. https://climateemergencyeu.org.

Chapter 11: 1 + 1 + 1 + . . . = ?

123 William MacAskill, *Doing Good Better: How Effective Altruism Can Help You Make a Difference* (New York: Gotham Books, 2015).

124 Thomas C. Schelling, *Micromotives and Macrobehavior* (New York: W.W. Norton & Co., 1978).

125 Please note: I am not saying that this rule is one that people actually apply. But, if they did, this is what would occur.

126 Paul Ormerod, *Butterfly Economics: A New General Theory of Social and Economic Behavior* (New York: Pantheon, 1998).

127 ACLU, "Tribute: The legacy of Ruth Bader Ginsburg and WRP staff." 2020. https://www.aclu.org/other/tribute-legacy-ruth-bader-ginsburg-and-wrp-staff.

128 Michael Gonchar and Shannon Doyne. "Justice Ginsburg fought for gender equality. How close are we to achieving that goal?" *New York Times*, September 20, 2020. https://www.nytimes.com/2020/09/20/learning/ruth-bader-ginsburg-equality-vision.html.

129 Positive Deviance Collaborative, "The Vietnam story: 25 years later."
April 14, 2018. https://positivedeviance.org/case-studies-all/2018/4/16/
the-vietnam-story-25-years-later. Mauricio L. Miller, *The Alternative:
Most of What You Believe About Poverty Is Wrong*. 2017. https://www.
thealternativebook.org.

130 Jo M. Wilmshurst, Brenda Morrow, Avril du Preez, David Githanga, Neil
Kennedy, and Heather J. Zar, "The African Pediatric Fellowship Program:
Training in Africa for Africans." *Pediatrics* 137(1) (2016): e20152741.
https://doi.org/10.1542/peds.2015-2741.

Postscript: The Future We Create

131 As corporations gained power, they craved more — and fought for it
in court. Eventually, they gained something never imagined in the US
Constitution: the idea of *corporate personhood*, which gave them the same
rights and protections afforded to human beings. But this was gained in
a way that never should have made it into law. An official court reporter
for the Supreme Court produced a short summary (called a "headnote")
in an 1886 case involving a railroad to attach to the Court's formal
decision, as is the custom. The headnote said the Court had, in effect,
ruled that corporations were "people." It hadn't. The court reporter had
either erred (there was no recording equipment in the day), inserted
his own interpretation of the Supreme Court ruling (he was a well-
trained lawyer but had a practice of interjecting his opinion into factual
reporting), or had been spoken to by a particular Supreme Court Justice
hearing the case who wanted to skew the report in favor of corporate
personhood (and so reap the railroad's patronage).

No matter: a court reporter's headnote carries no legal weight; only
official decisions do. But humans being human, we sometimes take
shortcuts, preferring ease over accuracy. And this includes lawyers.
So lawyers began to substitute the results in this brief summary for
the law itself. Which led to future cases being decided as if corporate
personhood actually were the law, and then even more cases being
decided based on those precedents.

There is also the possibility that a couple of the authors of the
Fourteenth Amendment — which was about slavery — intentionally
subverted it by using vague language ("person" rather than "natural
person") in hopes that, decades later, it might be interpreted as
conferring "personhood" on corporations (sometimes considered
"artificial persons"), which is exactly what happened. Or possibly the
same Justice who may have pushed the court reporter to write his

erroneous headnote then began to deliberately, and knowingly, refer to this misinterpretation in other legal decisions, to further cement it into law.

And so, through some combination of sloppiness, deception, manipulation, and corruption, corporations became people. See Thom Hartmann, *Unequal Protection: How Corporations became "People": and You Can Fight Back*. 2nd rev. edn. San Francisco: Berrett-Koehler Publishers, 2010. Also, Thom Hartmann, "Unequal protection: The deciding moment?" Truthout, April 8, 2011. https://truthout.org/articles/unequal-protection-the-deciding-moment.

132 Lee Drutman and Charlie Cray, *The People's Business: Controlling Corporations and Restoring Democracy* (Oakland, CA: Berrett-Koehler Publishers, 2004).

133 http://www.licensedtokill.biz/articles.pdf.

134 http://www.licensedtokill.biz/media/pro30417.html.

135 John Lewis, "Together, you can redeem the soul of our nation." *New York Times*, July 30, 2020. https://www.nytimes.com/2020/07/30/opinion/john-lewis-civil-rights-america.html.

Appendix 1: Shopping Apps

136 T.P.L. Nghiem and L.R. Carrasco, "Mobile applications to link sustainable consumption with impacts on the environment and biodiversity." *BioScience* 66(5) (2016): 384–92. https://academic.oup.com/bioscience/article/66/5/384/2468613.

Appendix 3: How to Support Local Business

137 Paul Egan, "Snyder signs bill ending incentives for film industry." *Detroit Free Press*, July 10, 2015. https://eu.freep.com/story/news/local/2015/07/10/snyder-signs-bill-ending-film-credits/29969583.

138 Louise Story, "As companies seek tax deals, governments pay high price." *New York Times*, December 1, 2012. https://www.nytimes.com/2012/12/02/us/how-local-taxpayers-bankroll-corporations.html.

139 Brian X. Chen, "Up to 91% more expensive: How delivery apps eat up your budget." *New York Times*, February 6, 2020. https://www.nytimes.com/2020/02/26/technology/personaltech/ubereats-doordash-postmates-grubhub-review.html.

140 Nathaniel Popper, "As diners flock to delivery apps, restaurants fear for their future." *New York Times*, June 9, 2020. https://www.nytimes.com/2020/06/09/technology/delivery-apps-restaurants-fees-virus.html.

141 Greg Bensinger, "Apps are helping to gut the restaurant industry." *New York Times*, December 8, 2020. https://www.nytimes.com/2020/12/08/opinion/delivery-apps-restaurants-fees.html.

142 Kimiko de Freytas-Tamura, "Food delivery apps are booming. their workers are often struggling." *New York Times*, November 30, 2020. https://www.nytimes.com/2020/11/30/nyregion/bike-delivery-workers-covid-pandemic.html.

143 Daniel M. West, "On Proposition 22, a big California victory for the gig economy." Brookings, November 4, 2020. https://www.brookings.edu/blog/techtank/2020/11/04/on-proposition-22-a-big-california-victory-for-the-gig-economy.

144 Laura Hayes, "An 8-month debrief: Can DC To-GoGo compete with big delivery services?" *Washington City Paper*, January 21, 2021. https://washingtoncitypaper.com/article/506351/an-8-month-debrief-can-dc-to-gogo-compete-with-big-delivery-services.

145 Kiss the Ground, *#EAT4CLIMATE: Purchasing Guide*. 2018. https://kisstheground.com/wp-content/uploads/2021/11/KTG_Purchasing_Guide_101718.pdf.

146 *Ibid.*

Appendix 4: Tools For Finding Effective Charities

147 Dylan Matthews, "Want to donate to charity? Here are 10 guidelines for giving effectively. How to do the most good possible with the money you give." *Vox*, November 29, 2021. https://www.vox.com/future-perfect/21728843/best-charities-donate-giving-tuesday.

148 Sigal Samuel and Muizz Akhtar, "Want to fight climate change effectively? Here's where to donate your money. These are seven of the most high-impact, cost-effective, evidence-based organizations. You may not have heard of them." *Vox*, November 30, 2021. https://www.vox.com/future-perfect/2019/12/2/20976180/climate-change-best-charities-effective-philanthropy.

Appendix 5: Tools for Finding Good Banks and Credit Unions

149 Alice Holbrook, "Fewer black-owned banks survive to fill vital financial needs." *NerdWallet*, February 6, 2018. https://www.nerdwallet.com/article/banking/black-owned-banks-fight-to-bounce-back.

Appendix 6: Tools for Responsible and Sustainable Investing

150 Brian Belley, "Top 10 equity crowdfunding sites — 2020." CrowdWise. org, September 13, 2020. https://crowdwise.org/funding-portals/ top-10-equity-crowdfunding-sites-2020.

151 WeFunder: https://wefunder.com
StartEngine: https://www.startengine.com
SeedInvest: https://www.seedinvest.com
Kiva: https://www.kiva.org
Republic: https://republic.com
Netcapital: https://netcapital.com
NextSeed: https://www.nextseed.com
MicroVentures: https://microventures.com
Credibles: https://credibles.co
Honeycomb Credit: https://www.honeycombcredit.com
Mainvest: https://mainvest.com
GrowthFountain: https://growthfountain.com/pg/business-tutorial
Crowdfund Mainstreet: https://crowdfundmainstreet.com
Mr. Crowd: https://www.mrcrowd.com
Small Change: https://www.smallchange.co
Wunderfund: https://www.wunderfund.co
Milk Money: https://milkmoneyinvesting.com
truCrowd: https://us.trucrowd.com
Gridshare: https://moixa.com/business-services
Rabble: https://rabble.capital
SVXUS: https://svxus.org
FlashFunders: https://www.flashfunders.com
Jumpstart Micro: https://jumpstartmicro.com
In Kind Direct: https://www.inkinddirect.org

Index